ARCHITECTS
OF POVERTY

Moeletsi Mbeki

ARCHITECTS
OF POVERTY

Why African Capitalism Needs Changing

PICADOR AFRICA

First published 2009 by Picador Africa,
an imprint of Pan Macmillan South Africa
Private Bag X19, Northlands
Johannesburg 2116

www.panmacmillan.co.za
www.picadorafrica.co.za

ISBN 978-1-77010-161-6

© Moeletsi Mbeki 2009

Editing by Pat Tucker and Andrea Nattrass
Proofreading by Sally Hines
Cover design and typesetting by Triple M Design, Johannesburg
Printed by Ultra Litho, Johannesburg

CONTENTS

FIGURES   vi

TABLES   vii

PREFACE   ix

ABBREVIATIONS   xiii

CHAPTER 1: Africa's Malaise   1

CHAPTER 2: South Africa's Elites   39

CHAPTER 3: The De-Industrialisation of South Africa   63

CHAPTER 4: The Making of a Failed African State   101

CHAPTER 5: The Failure of Regional Integration   131

CHAPTER 6: Africa Needs a New Democracy   151

APPENDIX: 'Gukurahundi'   177

NOTES   189

FIGURES

4.1 Zimbabwe's GDP Growth (1990–2008)   102

4.2 Zimbabwe's tobacco production (1990–2009)   104

4.3 Zimbabwean trade volumes (1990–2004)   105

4.4 The manufacturing sector as a portion of
Zimbabwe's GDP (1985–2008)   107

4.5 Zimbabwe's GDP income per capita (1965–2008)   123

4.6 South African trade with Zimbabwe (1994–2001)   123

6.1 Employment trends in South Africa and
elsewhere (1980–2006)   165

6.2 Breakdown of South Africa's merchandise
exports (1990–2005)   167

6.3 China's exports to South Africa (2004)   169

6.4 South Africa's exports to China (2004)   170

TABLES

1.1 Percentage of the labour force working in the
   agricultural, industrial and services sectors   13
1.2 Value added per worker in US$ in the
   manufacturing sector in Nigeria   26
5.1 Total intra-SADC trade (exports and imports)   143

PREFACE

The curator pointed to a large musket hanging on the wall – one of the items sold to Africans as part of the infamous Triangular Trade whereby manufactured goods were shipped from Europe to West Africa and exchanged for slaves, who were shipped to the Americas to grow sugar, cotton and tobacco that were then shipped back to Europe. This was mercantile capitalism in action.

With my South African mindset I queried the wisdom of European slavers selling guns to Africans: surely the guns would be turned on the Europeans, I ventured, betraying my ignorance about the workings of the African slave trade.

The curator, a patient professor from the University of

Dakar, explained that it was the Africans who caught the people in the interior and sold them to the owners of the ships that transported them to the Americas to be sold into slavery. So it was the Africans who needed the guns to protect themselves against the communities they raided for people to sell.

This little drama happened in the dingy Slave House on Gorée Island, off the coast of Dakar, the capital of Senegal.

The Slave House was, in reality, a prison-cum-warehouse, the ground floor of which was used to house Africans destined for enslavement in the Americas. Upstairs were the traders' quarters, linked to the ground floor by a dramatic staircase. The cupboard under the stairs served as a solitary confinement cell for 'difficult' slaves. The curator told me that tears had trickled down Nelson Mandela's cheeks when he was shown the isolation cell.

The Slave House is the only building on Gorée Island whose back door opens directly to the sea. It's known as 'the door of no return'. The people walking through the door onto waiting ships would never see their home country again.

Fast forward from the Slave House to the oil rigs along the Gulf of Guinea. One evening I flew from Lagos to northern Namibia along the gulf. Running the length of this amazing coastline are hundreds of oil rigs, rendered visible at night by the flames of the natural gas they flare. The rigs are not connected to the mainland; they pump crude oil from the bowels of the earth to waiting oil tankers – those ships again! – which carry the oil straight from the rigs to the great oil-refining industries in the United States, Asia and Europe; another commodity Africa is selling to the rest of the world. In the past it was its people; today it is its natural resources.

*　*　*

These two experiences are what led me to the central theme of this book – the way the powerful in Africa instead of enriching their societies sell off the continent's assets to enrich the rest of the world. In return for this service these powerful Africans – who I call the political elites – receive the crumbs from the tables of the foreigners who make their fortunes by processing Africa's resources.

What I have described, whether slave trade or oil trade, is known as mercantile capitalism. Mercantile capitalism is the earliest form of capitalism and its principle is buying cheap and selling dear. Capitalism in the West has moved a long way from the days of mercantile capitalism; it went through the stage of industrialisation and Western countries are now referred to as post-industrial societies.

The problem with Africa is that it is still locked in the mercantile stage of capitalism. The challenge facing the continent is how to modernise capitalism from mercantilism to industrialism. Two countries are an exception to this observation – South Africa and Mauritius.

Why don't the powerful in Africa ever learn that mercantilism is a road to nowhere? Africa needs new rulers – the people themselves – who understand that the path to a prosperous future lies in hard work, creativity, knowledge and equity.

Moeletsi Mbeki
Johannesburg
April 2009

ABBREVIATIONS

AME   African Methodist Episcopal (Church)

ANC   African National Congress

AU   African Union

BEE   Black Economic Empowerment

Codesa   Convention for a Democratic South Africa

Comesa   Common Market for Eastern and Southern Africa

Cosatu   Congress of South African Trade Unions

DRC   Democratic Republic of Congo

GDP   Gross Domestic Product

GNI   Gross National Income

GPA   Global Political Agreement

IDC   Industrial Development Corporation

IMF	International Monetary Fund
MDC	Movement for Democratic Change
MEC	Minerals-Energy Complex
MMD	Movement for Multi-Party Democracy
Nail	New Africa Investments Limited
Nepad	New Partnership for Africa's Development
OAU	Organization of African Unity
OECD	Organisation for Economic Co-operation and Development
PDI	Previously Disadvantaged Individual
PHR	Physicians for Human Rights
PF-Zapu	Patriotic Front – Zimbabwe African People's Union
SACU	Southern African Customs Union
SADC	Southern African Development Community
Zanla	Zimbabwe National Liberation Army
Zanu-PF	Zimbabwe African National Union – Patriotic Front
ZCTU	Zimbabwe Congress of Trade Unions

CHAPTER 1

AFRICA'S MALAISE

WHEN THE COLONIES IN AFRICA AND ASIA BECAME INDEPENDENT in the years between 1945 and 1965 their political leaders were faced with two main challenges. The first they thought was a short- to medium-term challenge – consolidating their political power and achieving domestic stability and peace. The second, which they believed would challenge them in the medium to long term, was how to transform their countries' economies from their colonial format as suppliers of raw materials produced through the exploitation by the colonialists of the cheap, unskilled (and de-skilled) labour of the indigenous populations.

The new political elites aspired to develop integrated

industrial economies that resembled those of the departing metropolitan powers; economies that would produce both raw materials and manufactured products using an indigenous labour force that was healthier, better educated and better clothed than it had been in colonial times.

The outcome of this mega project is today a matter of general knowledge. Asian countries experienced many bloody conflicts in the early years but, by 1965, most of these conflicts – with the exception of those in Indochina, where they continued well into the 1970s – had been resolved and the countries of East, South East and South Asia started on the second challenge – developing and diversifying their economies.

Africa's story is far more complex. Many old conflicts continue to this day, for example, those within the Sudan or between Ethiopians and Eritreans. New conflicts continue to erupt, on a scale and with a ferocity that is hard to fathom. Examples include the genocide in Rwanda and the internal conflict that, for all practical purposes, has split Côte d'Ivoire – once the crown jewel of West Africa – in two. On the economic front, with a few exceptions, Africa's political elites have driven their countries' economies backwards.

In its seminal review of economic and social conditions in sub-Saharan Africa at the dawn of the new century, *Can Africa Claim the 21st Century?*, the World Bank noted that it had been expected that Asia would remain mired in poverty while Africa would steam ahead. The opposite, however, has been the case. Comparing Ghana and South Korea, two countries that were at a similar level of development in the 1960s, the World Bank had this to say:

> In 1965, for example, incomes and exports per capita were higher in Ghana than in Korea. But projections proved to be far off the mark. Korea's exports per capita overtook Ghana's in 1972, and its income level surpassed Ghana's four years later. Between 1965 and 1995 Korea's exports increased by 400 times in current dollars. Meanwhile, Ghana's increased only by 4 times, and real earnings per capita fell to a fraction of their earlier value.[1]

Promising start and near collapse

The world has done just about everything it can to help Africa develop but there are few positive results to show for its efforts. While Asia forges ahead in the development stakes Africa is marking time at best, and, at worst, marching backwards.

It was not always so. In the 1960s, soon after their independence, many African countries did reasonably well and their economies grew quite significantly. It was an age of creativity, with universities and high schools sprouting throughout the continent, leading to vibrant debates about how to propel Africa forward.

In those years, when political elites were relatively small and were still close to the masses who had supported them in their struggles against colonialism, they made a great deal of effort not only to grow their countries' economies but also to distribute the benefits of growth to their peoples through investment in social and physical infrastructure.

This point is well demonstrated by the research of Thandika Mkandawire into the role of the state in economic development in Africa. Mkandawire writes:

> If one takes a growth rate of 6 per cent over more than a decade as a measure of successful development performance, in the 1967–1980 periods, ten countries enjoying such growth were African. These not only included mineral-rich countries such as Gabon, Botswana, Congo and Nigeria but also such countries as Kenya and Côte d'Ivoire, who slightly outperformed both Indonesia and Malaysia during the period. One interesting feature is that much of this growth was sustained largely by domestic savings, which increased significantly after independence, reaching, on the average 21.5 per cent by 1980.[2]

No sooner had the flame of Africa's potential success begun to be visible from a distance than it was extinguished. The first blow was the murder of Patrice Lumumba, first prime minister of the newly independent Democratic Republic of Congo (DRC),[3] followed by the overthrow of Ghana's Kwame Nkrumah by the army (with a little help from the United States government),[4] and the restriction of Oginga Odinga, Kenya's first vice-president and later opposition leader.[5] Africa soon descended to unimaginably low depths. Civil wars erupted in Nigeria, Algeria, Liberia, Sierra Leone, Angola and the two Congos, to name but a few, culminating in genocide in Rwanda and in failed and failing states in Somalia, Zimbabwe and Côte d'Ivoire. These conflicts caused untold suffering and massive destruction to already underdeveloped infrastructure.

Two primary factors drove many of these post-independence conflicts. The first was disagreements among the African nationalists over what economic and social policies to pursue. Many favoured continuing with the old colonial models minus the racial discrimination factor but some, among them Odinga and Nkrumah, described such policies as neo-colonialism and saw them as representing continued collaboration with the former Western colonial powers.

The second driver of conflict was the Cold War that raged

between the Western and communist powers from the end of the Second World War in 1945 to the collapse of the Berlin Wall in 1989. The Western liberal democratic pro-capitalist camp, which included Africa's former colonial masters, worked under the leadership of the United States to nurture an adherence to the West in the former colonies. This led to clashes with those elements among the African nationalist movements that either wanted to weaken Western influence or to strike out on their own third way under the name of non-alignment between capitalism and communism.

Understanding African nationalism

Nationalism in Africa has always paraded itself as a movement of the people fighting for their liberation. The reality is, in fact, rather different. African nationalism was a movement of the small, Westernised black elite that emerged under colonialism. Its fight was always for inclusion in the colonial system so that it, too, could benefit from the spoils of colonialism.

The colonial system was not designed to develop the productive capacities of the colonies. The driving motive of colonisation was to extract the continent's mineral and agricultural raw materials to be shipped to the mother countries for processing into manufactured goods. With this as their only aim, all the colonisers required from the colonised was a steady supply of unskilled labour – all skilled labour was shipped in from the metropole.

There was, however, a demand for local intermediaries such as court interpreters, teachers, medical orderlies and agricultural extension workers, who provided a line of communication between the colonisers and the colonised and transmitted some necessary skills, such as a knowledge of the European languages needed to follow the instructions of the colonialists. It was out of this group of educated intermediaries that the African nationalist movements emerged.

Independence did not bring about economic transformation in Africa as it did in Asia; if anything, it entrenched the economic inequalities inherited from colonialism. The new black elites merely replaced the former white colonial elites, but the exploitation of the black masses continued as before, as did the exploitation of Africa's resources – the copper, gold, bauxite, iron ore, cobalt, coltan, oil, timber, cotton, coffee, cocoa beans – drawn from the continent and exported to the rest of the world.

It is this drive to retain control over the continent's resources that goes some way to explaining the fear among nationalist-ruled southern African governments of new-age, people-created parties, such as Zimbabwe's Movement for Democratic Change (MDC). They fear that these parties will destroy the neo-colonial system off which they live. It also explains the support by states in the Southern African Development Community (SADC) for Robert Mugabe's regime, despite the havoc his actions are causing in neighbouring countries.

Once seen as a progressive and dynamic movement that would deliver Africa from bondage to modernity and prosperity, African nationalism has turned out to be a massive disappointment.

Half a century after its liberation from colonialism Africa has dropped so far down the development scale that experts refer to Africans as mankind's Bottom Billion, who can only come out of the black hole they have dug for themselves through intervention by the rest of the world.

There is no better illustration of the failure of African nationalism than Zimbabwe under the leadership of Zanu-PF (Zimbabwe African National Union – Patriotic Front) and its leader, Robert Mugabe. In the decade 1999–2009 Zimbabwe has shown how an African country can travel from relative prosperity to the status of basket case.

What went wrong?

What has gone wrong has been the massive mismanagement by Africa's ruling political elites, with the help of Western powers, of the economic surplus generated in Africa in the past 40 years. As heirs of the colonial state, political elites exploited their strong position in relation to the private sector – which, in Africa, comprises peasant and plantation agriculture, domestic and foreign-owned manufacturing industries and foreign-owned extractive industries – to:

❏ bolster their standards of living to levels comparable with those of the middle and upper classes of the West;
❏ undertake half-hearted, loss-making industrialisation projects that were not supported by the necessary technical and managerial educational development; and
❏ transfer vast amounts of economic surpluses generated by agriculture and extractive industries, such as oil, diamonds, metals and timber, to developed countries as capital flight, while simultaneously obtaining vast loans from developed countries.

Zimbabwe provides a textbook example of the relationship between the falling standards of living in sub-Saharan Africa and the growing power of political elites. In their struggle against the white minority regime, Zimbabwe's African nationalists enlisted, in particular, the support of the peasants and agricultural workers who constitute the majority of the population of that country.

During the 1980s, in the first decade of Zimbabwe's independence, the Zanu-PF government made strenuous efforts to uplift these constituencies. But it also set out to crush its former ally, PF-Zapu, which it succeeded in doing after a great deal of bloodletting. What remained of PF-Zapu was absorbed into Zanu-PF in 1987.

Once it had consolidated its hold on power the Zanu-PF political elite soon forgot about its wartime constituency and proceeded to enrich itself, to the great detriment of the national economy and of the welfare of the population at large. (For more about this process, see Chapter 4.)

Actions like this have ensured that most Africans in sub-Saharan Africa are poor and getting poorer. The World Bank and the International Monetary Fund, sub-Saharan Africa's fairy godparents, churn out statistics each year that tell the tale of this continuing drop in living standards.

With poverty and growing impoverishment go conflicts over scarce and shrinking resources. Hence, sub-Saharan Africa's apparently never-ending cycle of violent conflict.

In *Can Africa Claim the 21st Century?* the World Bank observes:

> Despite gains in the second half of the 1990s, Sub-Saharan
> Africa (Africa) enters the 21st century with many of the world's
> poorest countries. Average income per capita is lower than at

the end of the 1960s. Incomes, assets, and access to essential services are unequally distributed. And the region contains a growing share of the world's absolute poor, who have little power to influence the allocation of resources.[6]

These observations have been corroborated by other researchers. This was how the (United States) National Bureau of Economic Research summarised the living conditions of Africans:

Thirty-six per cent of the region's population lives in economies that in 1995 had not regained the per capita income levels first achieved before 1960. Another six per cent are below levels first achieved by 1970, 41 per cent below 1980 levels and 11 per cent below 1990 levels. Only 35 million people reside in nations that had higher incomes in 1995 than they had ever reached before.[7]

The key to economic development

All modern schools of political thought, from Karl Marx and Vladimir Lenin on the left to Friedrich Hayek and Milton Friedman on the right, agree on at least one thing: private entrepreneurship is the driver of modern economic development.

11

In a quest for greater security and comfort, the theory goes, private individuals and their households are driven to seek ever increasing material wealth. This process, in turn, compels these private individuals to produce more and more and exchange what they produce with other individuals who are also seeking greater security and comfort. The sum total of these acts of production, exchange and consumption constitute the modern capitalist economy. The capitalist economy is therefore inherently driven to produce more and more so that its denizens may increase their security and comfort.

If private individuals are to produce more and better goods they must generate savings which they plough back into the production process as new and improved techniques, processes and products. This enables these individuals to produce better and more diverse products to exchange with others who are doing the same.

This is the inexorable logic of capital accumulation. The more you produce the more you must produce, the cheaper you must produce and the better products you must produce, because, if you do not, others who are seeking greater security and comfort will displace you in the marketplace and you will therefore suffer reduced security and comfort. The keywords of this system are, therefore, production, exchange, markets, savings, improved techniques (research and development), medium of exchange (money) and economic growth.

Africans are, of course, no different from other human beings in desiring security and comfort. What is happening, however, is that the great majority of Africans are today experiencing the opposite – less security and comfort. In fact, in many instances they face hunger, homelessness, the threat of violence, actual violence, disease and starvation.

Africa today has arguably one of the largest private sectors in the world if we consider the peasant household as a firm. Most Africans live and work in the private households that populate the African countryside (see Table 1.1).

Table 1.1 **Percentage of the labour force working in the agricultural, industrial and services sectors**

	Agriculture			Industry			Services		
	1970	1980	1990	1970	1980	1990	1970	1980	1990
Agricultural countries									
Ethiopia	91	89	86	2	2	2	7	9	12
Kenya	84	82	80	5	6	7	9	11	13
Oil-producing countries									
Nigeria	71	54	43	11	8	7	19	38	50
Gabon	79	65	52	9	12	16	12	22	33
Newly industrialising countries									
Mauritius	34	27	17	25	28	43	41	45	40
South Africa	31	17	14	30	35	32	39	48	54

Source and ©: World Bank. 2002. *African Development Indicators 2002*.
  Washington, DC: World Bank.

Theoretically, if we refer to the model described above, Africa should be a hive of economic activity and growth driven by the logic of these private individuals and households attempting to maximise their security and comfort. What has gone wrong?

The underlying assumption of the model is that private individuals or entrepreneurs are free to pursue their search for security and comfort and that they therefore own and control the means of doing so. They are assumed to be free to exchange what they produce without let or hindrance and, where they are able to save, are free to retain those savings and plough them back into improving techniques or into other investment avenues.

Industrial and agrarian revolutions for Africa

But this is not the case in sub-Saharan Africa. Africa's private sector is predominantly made up of peasants and of subsidiaries of foreign-owned multinational corporations. Neither of these two groups has the freedom to operate in the market place because both are politically dominated by others – the non-producers who control the state. This explains the inability of Africa's private sector to become the engine of economic development. It lacks political power and is therefore not free to operate in such a way as to maximise its objectives. Above all, as already indicated, it is not free to decide what happens to its savings.

The indigenous people of the Americas and of Africa bore the brunt of European imperialism. From the late fifteenth century to the end of the nineteenth century systematic genocide was committed against the native peoples of North and South America and the Caribbean. Only recently have the few peoples who survived the carnage in the Andean states of Peru and Bolivia started to make their voices heard.

European imperialism was equally devastating for Africa. Vast numbers of people were taken off as slaves to the Americas. Massive intra-continental conflicts were generated by slave raiders, most of whom were, themselves, Africans. Equally importantly, Africa's indigenous manufacturing industries were systematically destroyed and their products replaced with cheap imports from Europe. Africa's arts and craft skills were thus adulterated, commercialised and, in some cases, obliterated. The continent was overwhelmed spiritually and intellectually by European imperialism, resulting in Africans abandoning their religions, which were marginalised, vulgarised and vilified by missionaries.

The story was somewhat different in Asia, where the negative impact of European imperialism was not as profound as it was in Africa. Although in the nineteenth century the British initially devastated India's traditional textile industry by importing machine-made cotton fabric from Manchester, Indian entrepreneurs hit back, acquiring modern technology and establishing their own textile companies. Asian religions – Islam, Buddhism and Hinduism – also proved to be impervious to the efforts of Christian missionaries.

Thus it was that the states the African political elites inherited from the colonialists were flawed to start with, imposed as they were by force and by foreigners. The colonialists used these states as instruments not only of political oppression but also of economic exploitation, through, for example, poll taxes and forced labour on plantations, mines and infrastructure projects. While poll taxes and forced labour in its many forms generated cheap labour, the introduction of cash crops provided the colonial state with forms of revenue and profit that were, in turn, used to consolidate the power of the colonisers over the colonised. Cash crops were bought from the peasants either by state corporations or by favoured private monopolies from the colonial power's home country. Either way, the farmers were paid prices far below those of the world market.

African political elites today sustain and reproduce themselves by perpetuating the neo-colonial state and its attendant socio-economic systems of exploitation, devised by the colonialists. The colonial model of exploitation was, however, parasitic on pre-capitalist African social systems and failed to transform Africa's largely subsistence modes of production though it introduced some modifications to enable the colonial powers to extract raw materials and small surpluses from these economic systems. These small surpluses were used to finance colonial administration infrastructures.

Sub-Saharan Africa today consists of fossilised pre-industrial and pre-agrarian-revolution social formations, and therein lies their inability to grow economically. The absence of an industrial revolution on the African sub-continent has left it with socio-economic structures that are, in the main, degenerative rather than accumulative.

The stunted subsistence economic systems established by the colonialists and perpetuated since their departure by successive groups of political elites were unable to absorb new technologies and new management methods. Over time, they began to eat up their own foundations, leading to the ills for which sub-Saharan Africa has became notorious – declining life expectancy, falling school enrolment, capital flight, the brain drain, deforestation, desertification, conflict, massive and growing inequality, endemic and growing poverty, manipulation by outside forces and a growing dependence on foreign patronage and on solutions initiated from outside the continent.

Sub-Saharan Africa also has no established and stable

social structure or stable ruling classes that are legitimate in the eyes of most of the citizens. It thus lacks a leadership with the continuity necessary to sustain and implement developmental economic programmes, a situation that is likely to persist for a long time to come because of the mass emigration of African professionals. The World Bank estimates that 20 000 African graduates leave the continent each year.[8]

The plight of the peasant

According to Marx, peasants are open to exploitation by other social groups, which dominate them politically, because they are unable to form an independent political force to represent their interests.

In one of the famous passages from his classic analysis of French society in the nineteenth century, Marx had this to say about the powerlessness and consequent vulnerability of peasants:

> The smallholding peasants form a vast mass, the members of which live in similar conditions but without entering into manifold relations with one another. Their mode of production isolates them from one another instead of bringing them into a mutual intercourse ... Each family is almost self-sufficient;

it itself directly produces the major part of its consumption and thus acquires its means of life more through exchange with nature than in intercourse with society. A smallholding, a peasant and his family; along side them another peasant and another family. A few score of these make up a village, and a few score of villages make up a Department ... In so far as millions of families live under economic conditions of existence that separate their mode of life, their interests and their culture from those of the other classes, and put them in a hostile position to the latter, they form a class. In so far as there is merely a local interconnection among these smallholding peasants, and the identity of their interests begets no community, no national bond and no political organisation among them, they do not form a class. They are consequently incapable of enforcing their class interests in their own name, whether through a parliament or through a convention. They cannot represent themselves, they must be represented.[9]

But who represents the interests of the peasants in Africa today? The answer is, 'nobody'. Africa's peasants are prey to forces with the ability to form political organisations and therefore to control the state.

A good example of this can be seen in Zimbabwe, where Robert Mugabe, the one African politician who claims to act in the interests of peasants, has reduced once proud and almost self-sufficient Zimbabwean peasants to paupers who have to be fed by the United Nations World Food Programme.

The way in which peasants are preyed upon by those who control the state – the political elites – has been studied extensively, not least by the World Bank itself.[10] Fundamentally, political elites use their control of the state to extract any surplus or savings peasants might have invested in improving their production techniques or diversifying into other economic activities. Through marketing boards, taxation systems and the like, political elites divert these savings to finance their own consumption and to strengthen the repressive instruments of the state.

The Economist makes the following observation about Ethiopia's dependence on foreign food donations: 'By law, all Ethiopian land is owned by the state. Farmers are loath to invest in improving productivity when they have no title to the land they till. Nor can they use land as collateral to raise credit. And they are taxed so heavily that they rarely have any surplus cash to invest.'[11]

A great deal of what Africa's political elites and African states consume is, however, not produced locally but is imported. Elite and state consumption, therefore, does not create a significant market for African producers but instead

20

acts as a major drain on national savings which might otherwise have gone into productive investment.

One of the most striking illustrations of this phenomenon is the case of Nigeria. According to a study prepared by the Centre for the Study of African Economies at Oxford University, between 1980 and 2000 per capita Gross Domestic Product (GDP) (in 1996 US$ purchasing power parity terms) fell from US$1 215 to US$706. The authors of the study point out that growth and poverty are very closely related and that the 40 per cent drop in purchasing power parity understates the size of Nigeria's problem.

'First the fall in real per capita consumption was very much greater while the available evidence suggests that inequality rose. This combination of a very large fall in per capita consumption combined with increasing inequality implies a large rise in poverty.'[12] According to another source, the number of Nigerians living below the poverty line increased from 19 million in 1970 to 90 million in 2000. This increase was accompanied by a massive rise in inequality. In 1970 the top 2 per cent of the population earned the same income as the bottom 17 per cent, but, by 2000, the income of the top 2 per cent was equal to that of the bottom 55 per cent.[13]

To understand what might be achieved in Africa if the correct policies were in place let us compare what is happening in Nigeria with what is happening in China. While per capita

GDP nearly halved in Nigeria and the number of people living below the poverty line skyrocketed between 1970 and 2000, in China income per head increased sevenfold during the same period, lifting more than 400 million people out of poverty.[14]

The most graphic illustration of the iron law of African underdevelopment is the role played by the oil industry in oil-rich countries such as Nigeria, Libya, Algeria and Angola. Oil revenues make it possible for the political elite to become detached from the local population and the economy and therefore to live in an oasis. When this happens there is no need for the elite and the state it controls to invest in the mass education, healthcare, housing and transportation infrastructure that the population at large needs. The result is that countries lapse into a state of decay.

This is how, in a 2003 article, *The Economist* describes the impact of oil production on Equatorial Guinea and Gabon:

> Equatorial Guinea now pumps more oil per person than Saudi Arabia. Its economy, once negligible, has grown at an incredible 40% annually since 1996, when the oil boom began. A few years ago, the streets of the capital, Malabo, were as quiet as São Tomé's are today. Now, Malabo's pretty Spanish colonial architecture bristles with satellite dishes, and the streets, bathed at night in an orange glow from gas flared at a nearby methanol plant, are gaudy with sports

cars, tropical palaces and prostitutes who flutter in from nearby countries such as Cameroon. And the tiny country's agriculture is blighted: cocoa and snail farmers have rushed to the towns to grab a slice of the oil bonanza.

Equatorial Guinea was never well-governed: Obiang Nguema, the president, seized power by executing his uncle in 1979. But oil has made his regime increasingly paranoid. Several members of the ruling family are thought to want a bigger slurp at the oil barrel. Mr Obiang sees plots everywhere, and arranged periodic crackdowns. Several opposition leaders were jailed last year after a mass trial, to which many defendants turned up with broken arms and legs. Mr Obiang scoffs at western notions of transparency, insisting that how much money his government earns from oil is nobody's business. 'Oil has turned him crazy,' says Celestino Bacale, a brave opposition politician.

In next-door Gabon, Omar Bongo has been in power since 1967. He is more subtle than Mr Obiang. He does not torture his enemies but buys them off. Decades of oil revenues have corrupted Gabonese society and eroded the work ethic. Citizens aspire to soft billets in the civil service, and turn their noses up at menial jobs like taxi driving or shopkeeping, which they leave to immigrants from poorer places such as Togo and Mali. Agriculture in Gabon, as in Equatorial Guinea, is all but dead.[15]

The vulnerability of multinational corporations

European joint stock companies have operated in Africa since the dawn of the capitalist era, their activities including the financing, insurance and operation of the ships that transported slaves to the New World. One of the most famous of them, the Dutch East India Company, started the colonisation of South Africa in the mid-seventeenth century. With the emergence of colonialism proper after the 1884 Berlin Conference, similar companies followed closely on the heels of the colonialists' conquering armies, establishing agricultural plantations, mines, railways, harbours and new cities. Later they diversified into creating consumer goods for the burgeoning African market, from soap and beer to blankets, fishing nets, the processing of raw materials, and so on.

When the colonialists retreated, from the 1950s onwards, these colonial subsidiaries lost their key protector, the colonial state. Before long they, like the peasants, fell prey to the appetites and whims of the political elites who controlled the newly independent African states. Some companies were fortunate to be nationalised and their owners paid compensation. One of these was the Anglo American Corporation of South Africa, whose copper mines were nationalised by the Zambian government in 1968. The company used the compensation to establish its international business based in the Bahamas.

The less fortunate ones were 'privatised' – confiscated by individual politicians who paid no compensation. This was what happened to many private businesses owned by Indian, Lebanese and Chinese entrepreneurs in countries such as Uganda, under Idi Amin, or Zaire, now the DRC, under Mobutu Sese Seko. In 1972, Amin expelled tens of thousands of ethnic Indians who dominated the country's economy. While the move was initially popular, the eviction of most of its entrepreneurs plunged Uganda into economic chaos.[16]

Many foreign businesses survived as best they could by corrupting the new elite or finding ways of ingratiating themselves with their new masters. In some Western countries companies got tax breaks if they were able to bribe African government officials.

Even the mighty Western oil companies have not escaped the destructive power of Africa's political elites and are periodically compelled to make huge payments into the foreign private bank accounts of the heads of state – and their families and friends – of oil-producing countries. The United States Senate has uncovered, for instance, vast sums paid by oil companies into the private bank accounts in Washington, DC, of Equatorial Guinea's head of state.[17]

What is most striking about the political elites in sub-Saharan Africa is their aversion to becoming involved in industry, whether manufacturing or mining, or in agriculture.

The private sector and entrepreneurship in general is therefore still dominated by foreign-owned companies, with parastatals playing an increasingly minor role.

A 2002 study by the World Bank shows that the most productive companies in, for example, Nigeria, are those owned by multinational corporations or by non-African industrialists – Indians, Chinese, Lebanese, and so on (see Table 1.2).

Table 1.2 **Value added per worker in US$ in the manufacturing sector in Nigeria**

Local	3 137.52
Foreign	8 790.12
Indigenous	4 460.05
Non-African	7 791.56
Micro	2 765.58
Small	3 859.39
Medium	5 020.36
Large	4 198.73
Very large	11 094.26

Source and ©: World Bank. 2002. *An Assessment of the Private Sector in Nigeria.* Washington, DC: World Bank.

These owners are easy targets as they are not represented within the political elites. Together with the peasants they are therefore subject to a range of official and unofficial taxes ranging from backhanders for factory inspectors and customs officials to artificially high electricity tariffs and arbitrary municipal rates.

This is another way in which African political elites contribute to fostering the continent's underdevelopment. With their operations obstructed and much of their profits diverted to elite consumption and to capital flight, Africa's manufacturing industries are unable to grow – with in many countries a trend towards de-industrialisation – and therefore are unable to create employment.

According to Eboe Hutchful, a Ghanaian researcher, his country's economy was in 'free fall' before 1983, when the World Bank came to the rescue:

> Between 1970 and 1980 per capita GDP declined by a total of 19,7%; from 1980 to 1983 it dropped by a further 21,3%. There was sharp decline in both domestic and export production. The manufacturing index plunged from 100 in 1977 to 69,0 in 1980 and 63,3 in 1981, with average capacity utilisation in that year estimated at only 24%.[18]

Even after a decade of the World Bank and other donors trying to breathe life into Ghana's industry after 1983 'overall capacity utilization improved from 30% in 1983 to 40% in 1989 and appears to have stagnated at around this level for much of industry in the 1990s', writes Hutchful.

The result of this massive onslaught against Africa's manufacturing and mining sectors and of their being deprived of investment funds are all too predictable. In a 2004 report the United Nations Industrial Development Organization (UNIDO) painted a grim picture of sub-Saharan Africa's de-industrialisation since 1970:

> Sub-Saharan Africa, as a whole, has *deindustrialized* since 1970, though there are a number of exceptions to this trend. Moreover, average manufacturing labour productivity relative to aggregate labour productivity is lower now than it was in 1970. There is, therefore, both a widening productivity gap between agriculture and manufacturing and between manufacturing and economy-wide productivity, meaning that sub-Saharan Africa has moved backwards in the past three decades.[19]

These factors do not mean that there has been no new investment in sub-Saharan Africa. Far from it. Investment in petroleum and other extractive industries proceeds apace. More recently, there has been a spate of investment in mobile telecommunications and in some tourism and retail infrastructure. A few new investors have also entered the field, in particular, South African and Mauritian corporations and companies from Asia and Latin America. These investments, however, do not make a significant dent in the continent's underdevelopment, especially since most investors shy away from long-term involvement in manufacturing.

The effects of long-term underinvestment

After independence African leaders hoped they would build a modern Africa with thriving industries, universities and hospitals. With a couple of exceptions, such as South Africa and Mauritius, this did not happen. Today Africa is littered with abandoned industrial parks. A few kilometres south of Lusaka, Zambia, is the industrial town of Kafue, once a hive of activity, today a ghost town. It had textile, fertiliser and chemical plants and a railway line that serviced these industries.

Zambia is not the only country with nothing to show for its post-independence modernisation drive. I once visited an aluminium smelter in Nigeria's Niger Delta that had been built at an estimated cost of US$2.5 billion. At the time of the visit the plant employed 800 people but did not produce a single kilogram of aluminium. The place, which has a 1 kilometre-long conveyer belt, its own port and its own power station linked by a 100 kilometre-long gas pipeline to an oil rig, had become a year-long holiday resort for its highly qualified and highly paid employees. Years later it was sold to a Russian oligarch for a fraction of what it cost to build.

One of the greatest scandals after decades of underinvestment in Africa is the state of the continent's transportation infrastructure. Virtually all the railway lines that were in use when the colonialists left sub-Saharan Africa between 40 and 50 years ago have long ceased to operate, or are operating at a fraction of their design capacity. If arch imperialist Cecil John Rhodes were to return from the grave he would be shocked to find that his highly achievable dream of a railway line running from Cape Town to Cairo is further away now than it was 100 years ago.

If we exclude those in South Africa, the only new railways that have been constructed in Africa in the past half-century were built by the Chinese. Africa is a vast continent, with most of its people living in its cooler interior, which is also where its substantial mineral resources, with the exception of petroleum, are found. By now it should be criss-crossed by railways going in all directions, linking neighbouring countries to one another and all countries to the coast. Instead, the continent has a decayed railway, port and road infrastructure that has stifled the development of mining and the expansion of agriculture. It is one of the many consequences of underinvestment. Others consequences of underinvestment are:

❑ Unable to find employment, Africa's people start migrating from country to country and eventually masses of skilled, semi-skilled and unskilled people cross the oceans to Europe.

❑ In order to keep their governments running in the face of declining revenues Africa's elites borrow from abroad to make up for revenue shortfalls, thus increasing their countries' indebtedness to international financiers and to foreign governments.

❑ In time African governments are unable to service their debts so they become dependent on gifts or donations from the governments of wealthy countries or from whoever wants to exploit Africa's rich natural resources.

High indebtedness and aid dependence thus become two sides of the some coin – economic stagnation. African countries have been stagnating for the past 40 years and there is no end in sight.

The dangers of donor dependence

Why is it that the more aid poured into Africa the poorer Africans seem to get?

Countries develop primarily by pooling the collective strengths and energies of their citizens to achieve a common objective. In order for citizens to do so, however, two key elements must be present – institutions that facilitate cooperation and leaders who ensure that these institutions function and deliver on expectations.

If individuals or households are expected to pool their energies and resources with other individuals or households there must be a mechanism that makes it possible and desirable for them to cooperate – the benefits of cooperation must outweigh those of working in isolation. Similarly, the costs of working in cooperation with others must be lower than those of working alone. In short, if cooperation is to be voluntary there must be incentives to encourage it.

Among these incentives are fairness, justice and rewards, so institutions that make cooperation possible must also deliver equity and social justice.

This is where leadership comes in. Social institutions such as political parties, religious organisations, private and public corporations, as well as sport and cultural organisations are created by many circumstances, but if they are to deliver fairness and equity their ways of operating must be constantly modified and adjusted. As circumstances change new ways of cooperating must be found by means of trial and error, and trial and error necessitate risk-taking, inherent in which is the possibility of failure and the cost, including the pain, of failure.

It is here that post-colonial Africa has come unstuck; it has failed both to develop new institutions of cooperation among its citizens and to produce the type of leaders required to take society forward in an ever-changing global environment.

The massive social, economic and political upheavals in Africa from the mid-1960s to the mid-1990s, when elements of multi-party democracy began to appear on the continent, destroyed a key indigenous African institution – the African nationalist party – leaving Africans atomised and therefore stranded without indigenous, legitimate institutions of cooperation to advance their interests. These upheavals also destroyed many of the leaders who had mobilised the African people to cooperate in the struggle against colonialism.

The institutions that were left standing and prospered during the era of dictatorship and one-party rule (in practice, one-man rule) were created by colonialism – the state, the military and police, the Western- and foreign-controlled private sector. These were the institutions that were recaptured from the African nationalists by the dictators and their Western backers before the nationalists could change them. The extensive privatisation of parastatals such as telephone companies, railway companies, airlines and broadcasters are cases in point. The dictators once more used these colonial institutions to impose on the African people the interests of the West and those of the dictators and their associated elites and cliques.

The notion that Africa 'works' because the corrupt, nepotistic and unaccountable Big Men who rule it reflect its traditional cultural practices could not be further from the truth – in reality those Big Men were the creation of neo-colonialism and the Cold War.

Africa's era of dictatorships and one-man rule was simultaneously the heyday of Western donor interventions on the continent. The two elements worked in partnership, reinforcing each other, with the central objective of destroying both indigenous, autonomous institutions and leaders who tried to promote any cooperation among Africans that was devoted to advancing the interests of the African people (and not Western interests). The structural adjustment programmes promoted by the World Bank, the International Monetary Fund and Western donors since the early 1980s were foreign interventions by the West that undermined the development of Africa's social institutions.[20]

Donor-created democracy

Africa's challenge today is that while the era of dictatorship has apparently ended, African countries do not, as yet, have indigenous institutions and leaders to promote cooperation among their citizens. Developing such institutions is a difficult, costly and lengthy business made even more complex by the fact that re-democratisation in Africa from the mid-1990s was brought about to a significant extent in countries such as Kenya and Malawi by the intervention of Western donors rather than primarily by the pro-democracy actions of African organisations or parties. The main exceptions to this general rule are Uganda and Rwanda, and possibly Nigeria.

A second factor is that during the three to four decades of dictatorship and neo-colonialism Africa suffered a massive brain drain, capital flight and the deterioration of infrastructure. Not surprisingly, democratic Africa no longer has the skilled and experienced people necessary to make it more productive. The civil service on the continent is notorious for its incompetence, not to mention its corruption. Most African countries also do not have popular institutions with the influence to combat the slide back to dictatorships and unconstitutional practices.

Thirdly, during the era of dictatorship Africa's manufacturing sector continued to be dominated by Western multinational corporations and by business owned by non-Africans – Indian, Arab, Chinese, and so on. Dictators stifled the growth of an indigenous entrepreneurial class, which they saw as a potential threat to their power. Even the state-owned enterprises (parastatals) established during the short-lived nationalist era were either sold off at the instigation of donors or transformed rapidly into centres of corruption

35

rather than centres of training for future indigenous entre-preneurs and managers.

Consequently, despite the recent euphoria in the World Bank and other organisations about Africa's economic growth, related to the commodity boom between 2001 and 2007, the reality is that Africa today is going through a period of de-industrialisation and becoming more dependent on the export of raw materials. Even countries such as South Africa and Zimbabwe, which had achieved a significant degree of industrialisation, are de-industrialising. The Zimbabwe economy has halved since 2000, while South Africa's manufacturing sector has declined from 25 per cent of GDP in 1990 to 16 per cent today. China's manufacturing sector, by contrast, is about 45 per cent of GDP, while India's is 25 per cent.[21]

So, can Africa meet its development challenges in current political circumstances? Historically, only societies with an independent middle class with significant scientific knowledge and managerial skills have produced a modernising political leadership. Among the origins of such a middle class were:

❏ well-travelled merchants, independent artisans and scholars in feudal societies; and
❏ ethnic minorities, such as the Jews in parts of Europe or the Parsee in India.

36

It is normally such middle strata – which occupy the space between the traditional ruling classes and the majority of the people, usually the rural masses – that drive social change, especially economic and political modernisation.

Africa does not, on the whole, have this independent middle stratum. It was a class that rose briefly during the colonial era and pioneered the anti-colonial struggle, but with a few exceptions this class was decimated after independence, during the era of dictators and donors.

Kenya provides a graphic illustration of the use of assassination to destroy leaders of the middle strata who questioned the neo-colonial agenda. Within a few years of independence several progressive Kenyans – Tom Mboya, Pio Pinto, J.M. Kariuki and Robert Ouko, to name but a few – died in 'mysterious circumstances'.[22]

Africa's development crisis could, therefore, be described as one of the non-emergence or, more accurately, the slow and frustrated emergence of an independent middle stratum from the mid-1960s to the present. The question 'can Africa solve its development challenges?' could thus be posed in another way. Is a new middle class emerging in Africa that can provide the leadership required to drive the continent's industrial and agrarian revolutions in the face of foreign interventions that foster the continent's traditional role in the world economy as a source of raw materials and cheap labour?

There is very little evidence that this is happening. Apart from the brain drain, the story of Africa today is the resurgence of the scramble for natural resources, but this time by both West and East. Africa is benefiting to some extent from this new scramble by way of higher commodity prices, increased royalties, new sources of no-strings-attached foreign aid and soft loans. But this will not necessarily lead to a solution to the continent's development challenges; it merely entrenches, as in the past, a parasitic bureaucratic bourgeoisie living off state revenues.

As competition between West and East for resources intensifies, Africa is likely to be caught in a second cold war – a war over resources. Predictably, this will lead to a new cycle of 'hot' conflicts on the continent. This is already happening in the Niger Delta over petroleum and in the Eastern DRC over coltan (columbite-tantalite, a metallic ore used extensively in electronic devices such as cellular telephones).

Mineral resource endowment and exploitation, as has been pointed out repeatedly, does not necessarily lead to economic and social development. It often does the opposite. The most developed mineral economy in Africa is that of South Africa, but even South Africa's extensive mining industry may, in the end, contribute to that country's de-industrialisation. Before exploring this phenomenon, however, let us look at the key players involved, South Africa's elites.

CHAPTER 2

SOUTH AFRICA'S ELITES

WHEN THE BRITISH EVENTUALLY CONQUERED ALL THE INDEPENDENT communities in South Africa by crushing the Boer Republics in 1901 they gained free rein over the country's mineral resources, especially the gold deposits of the Transvaal.

The British, however, soon realised that their victory over the Boers was something of a poisoned chalice since it did not give them access to the vast cheap labour they required to exploit the gold deposits. To recoup the massive investment they had made in fighting the Boers they imported labourers from China, but they knew this was only a short-term solution as both white and black South Africans would soon oppose these importations.

The long-term solution was to mobilise rural Africans both in South Africa and in the rest of southern Africa to supply labour for the mines, agriculture and the development of a transport infrastructure.

Faced with this challenge, in 1903 the British established the South African Native Affairs Commission, which, for nearly two years, criss-crossed southern Africa investigating potential threats from Africans to the new colony as well as opportunities for labour supplies. So were born the Witwatersrand Native Labour Association (Wenela), which recruited black miners from outside South Africa, and the Native Recruitment Corporation (NRC) – later renamed Teba – which recruited men inside South Africa.

In the brief five years from the signing of the Peace of Vereeniging in 1902 to the establishment of responsible government in the Transvaal and Orange River colonies in 1907 the British set South Africa on a political, economic and social trajectory that has survived virtually intact to this day. How did this happen?

The strategies the British put in place in those years and which have looked after their interests in South Africa for 100 years were, of course, not a stroke of genius; they were the result of a century of experience in ruling South Africa since they first took over the Cape from the Dutch in 1795.

Twentieth-century elites

At the beginning of the twentieth century, after the Anglo-Boer War, South Africa had three elites:

❑ the English commercial elite;
❑ the Afrikaner elite; and
❑ the African elite.

In their years ruling South Africa the British came to understand that they could not manage the affairs of the country without the participation of these elites, who they saw as potential allies.

What was important about these elites was that they were all creations of the colonial and capitalist system and therefore saw their interests as served by the entrenchment of that system. This is what distinguished the modern elites in South Africa and, indeed, in the whole of sub-Saharan Africa, from modern elites in Asia, which are a continuation of pre-colonial elites. Asian elites, even in communist countries such as China and Vietnam, have their roots in their countries' pre-colonial societies and therefore have experience and values that are centuries old. In China, descendants of the Mandarin class continued to play a major role in the creation of, for example, the Chinese Communist Party and

41

the nationalist Kuomintang. Similarly, in India the modern elites were members of the Brahmin class. Consequently, even where Asian elites embraced the capitalist system they created their own version rather than reproducing the colonial capitalist model, as was the case in South Africa and in most of Africa.

The English commercial elite

As relative newcomers to South Africa, drawn there from 1820 onwards by different circumstances, there was little cohesion within the English commercial elite and they had no independent political power base to speak of. The most powerful among them, such as the Randlords, represented mining investors in the city of London.

Elements of this group thus had economic power, but this did not translate into political power, as the Jameson Raid and its outcome showed. In 1895 the Randlords (known as Uitlanders) tried to organise an insurrection in Johannesburg against the Boer Transvaal Republic government in partnership with the forces sent by the British South Africa Company to subdue Rhodesia. This became known as the Jameson Raid, and it was defeated by the Boers. Consequently, the economic rights of the English commercial elite had to be underwritten by the British government, and this group could not be an independent political force.

The Afrikaner elite

It was a completely different story with the Afrikaner and the African elites, both of which had the potential to be formidable independent political players. To the British this meant either or both of these elites were potential allies in managing South Africa on behalf of British commercial interests. The problem for the British was that the Afrikaner elite, especially the frontiersmen of the Transvaal and the Orange Free State, saw their interests as antagonistic to those of the African elite. The British, therefore, had to make a choice and they chose the Afrikaners.

Several factors led to this choice. Firstly, the Afrikaner elite, the core of whom, as frontiersmen, had conquered South Africa, had military capacity, which they had demonstrated during the Anglo-Boer War. Secondly, the frontiersmen had the capacity to establish and manage a state as they had proved by establishing the Boer Republics. Lastly, but most importantly to British commercial interests, they had a long history of oppressing Africans and exploiting their labour. In the era of gold mining, these skills were at a premium.

However, the Afrikaner elite also presented a number of problems for the British. Firstly, they had the potential to align themselves with Britain's enemies, especially the Germans, Russians, French and Americans, as they had tried to do during the Anglo-Boer War. At the turn of the twentieth century British naval power was, however, such that Britain could contain such a threat. Secondly, and more importantly, was the fact that within the Afrikaner elite there were a number of clearly defined factions, some of which might pose problems for British interests.

After the Anglo-Boer War three main factions emerged among the Afrikaner elite: the accommodationist faction, which was willing to negotiate with the British, led by ex-Boer War Generals Louis Botha and Jan Smuts; the nationalist faction, most prominently represented by General J.B.M. Hertzog; and the diehard Bittereinders (literally, 'bitter-enders', those who were willing to fight to the bitter end), led by Generals De la Rey and De Wet.

The British gambled on the strength and staying power of the accommodationists. As the British army and navy continued to be based in South Africa for many years after 1907 this was an insurance policy that would become useful from time to time when the power of the accommodationists was challenged, for example, by the Bittereinders in 1914 and by white workers in 1913 and 1922.

The African elite
The African elite at the start of the twentieth century had none of the strengths the British wanted but did have several vulnerabilities, which made them a potential weak link.

The old aristocratic elite that had ruled African societies and led the resistance to colonisation was physically annihilated by the British in the nineteenth century. The African elite that existed at the turn of the twentieth century was, therefore, new. It had emerged during the colonial era as part of the British colonial project and consisted of the acculturated and Christianised elites that had arisen in the Cape and the colonies, promoted first by missionaries and later by the British government as valuable allies in military campaigns to defeat the independent tribes.

The African elite, like the Afrikaner elite, had its factions but, unlike those of the Afrikaner elite, there were only two: the accommodationist faction and a weaker nationalist faction. The accommodationist faction saw itself as an ally of the British and hoped the British would reciprocate. The nationalist faction, which, at the start of the twentieth century, was believed by the British to be under the strong influence of black Americans, especially the African Methodist Episcopal (AME) Church, never gained much ground.

Drivers of change in twentieth-century South Africa

The rise and fall of Afrikaner nationalism
From the brief outline above it is clear that the forces that

shaped South Africa during most of the twentieth century were primarily British capital and the Afrikaner elite, especially the nationalist faction. The National Party in reality ruled South Africa for most of the twentieth century after South Africa's independence in 1910. It first came to power in 1924 and, with the exception of a few years during the Second World War, only left power in 1994. The British were primarily interested in South Africa's minerals, especially diamonds and gold. To a lesser extent they were drawn to the supply to the domestic South African market of consumer goods and financial services in cooperation with the English commercial elite.

The Afrikaner elite to which the British handed state power in 1910 on the formation of the Union of South Africa was a class of property owners, latifundists who owned vast tracts of largely undeveloped land. In order to develop the land they needed cheap and plentiful labour, markets, transport to markets, finance and knowledge, and they used state power to address these needs. They already had the labour, in the form of labour tenants and sharecroppers who had settled on their farms. The new gold-mining towns provided the markets.

When the Afrikaner elite took over the South African government in 1910 the country was, in economic terms, a typical economically undeveloped African colony. By the time this group handed over power to the African elite 84 years later, the country had undergone an industrial revolution.

The Afrikaner elite was primarily interested in state power and in using that power to advance its economic interests, particularly its agricultural interests, and to develop an Afrikaner professional class to provide the skills required by the public and parastatal sectors. The upliftment of poor whites was part of the effort to create a supervisory, managerial and technical class.

In order to achieve its economic objectives, the Afrikaner elite promoted the emergence of state-owned enterprises such as the Electricity Supply Commission (Escom, now Eskom), the South African Railways and Harbours Corporation (SAR & H, now Transnet), the Land Bank, the South African Broadcasting Corporation (SABC), the Iron and Steel Corporation (Iscor, now Mittal), the Independent Development Corporation (IDC), the telecommunications provider Telkom, the Development Bank of South Africa (DBSA), the Armaments Corporation of South Africa (Armscor) and the South African Coal, Oil and Gas Corporation (Sasol).

The various state-owned enterprises were, however, largely dependent on loans and technology imported from the United Kingdom. Thus, for most of the twentieth century British commercial interests (later opened up to other Western investors), the Afrikaner elite and English commercial elite shared common interests. Investors in the mineral resources sector and the Afrikaner elite, who were major players in the grain production sector, especially maize and wheat, had a common agenda – to promote a cheap supply of labour.

* * *

A century of political discourse dominated by issues of race and ethnicity has led most South Africans to think of politics as independent of social structure. Nearly half a century of apartheid convinced many people that it is (race) consciousness and other ideologies rather than socio-economic structures that determine politics.

A leading proponent of this view was the late Andrew Asheron, who argued that while capitalism was dominant in South Africa at the social and political level, what ultimately inhibited the further development of the capitalist economy was the racial division of society, which was fostered by the Afrikaner state. He claimed that even the powerful capitalist stratum – 'mining magnates and English speaking politicians' – had to submit to this particular form of social organisation.[1]

Asheron attributed the extra-economic power of the Afrikaner state to 'an historical process whereby race discrimination, prejudice and ideology has, at one level, cut

48

loose from its original economic and political functional aspects to become an autonomous entity which in itself circumscribes any movement towards reforms by the white elite'. In other words, ideology (racism) was the final determinant on which further social change depended.

Since 1969, when the above exposition was made and became conventional wisdom, there have been significant changes in South Africa. Afrikaner nationalism self-destructed, as did the Afrikaner state, which Asheron had believed was practically immutable.

What happened? Why did Afrikaner nationalism succeed when it did and fail when it did?

It succeeded because it found a formula to deliver South Africa's vast mineral resources to world markets at competitive prices. Equally importantly, Afrikaner nationalism was able to deliver the mineral resources with a minimum use of violence against the labour force. And it failed when it could no longer deliver the mineral resources without the increasing use of violence against the labour force.

Two things happened. When Afrikaner nationalism had the right formula for delivering to world markets it received the qualified support and cooperation of both domestic and foreign owners of capital, especially mining capital, but also that of the multinational corporations invested in the manufacturing and financial services sectors.

From the mid-1970s onwards, however, the re-emergence of militant trade unionism amongst the black labour force resulted in the increasing use of force to deliver labour to capital. Not only did this disrupt production processes, it turned international public opinion against South Africa and led a growing movement for sanctions in member countries of the Organisation for Economic Cooperation and Development (OECD), an international organisation helping governments to tackle the economic, social and governance challenges of a globalised economy.

Gradually sections of domestic capital also started withdrawing their support from the nationalists and demanding changes in industrial relations legislation. By the mid-1980s domestic capital had opened discussions with exiled political parties in an effort to identify a replacement for Afrikaner nationalism.

These initiatives culminated in the refusal of American banks to roll over South African loans and, after public campaigns, the United States Congress passed the Comprehensive Anti-Apartheid Act over a veto by then President Ronald Reagan. Both international and local pressure ultimately resulted in the legalisation of banned political parties, the release of their leaders from prison and the return of others from exile.

* * *

From this brief description of what led to the demise of Afrikaner nationalism, it should be clear that it was the major social forces that constitute present-day South Africa's social structure, in particular, organised labour, big business and foreign investors, which finally destroyed it. Of course, many prominent individuals and political parties played their role in the drama, but their efforts were effective only because of the antagonism of the dominant forces in the country's social structure.

Despite these growth limitations, at the end of the era of the Afrikaner elite, in the early 1990s, South Africa had the strongest and largest economy in Africa, standing in relation to Africa where the United States stood in relation to the rest of the world. The United States, with 4.6 per cent of the world's population, accounted for 21.5 per cent of the world's Gross National Income (GNI); South Africa, with 5.5 per cent of Africa's population, accounted for 26.6 per cent of the continent's GNI.

South Africa's Industrial Revolution

Development analysts have pondered long and hard over why some countries develop and others do not. There is no mystery about what a country needs to do in order to develop, the imponderable is why some countries do what must be done and others do not. South Africa provides us

51

with something of a controlled experiment in this regard.

The reasons for the strength of the South African economy compared to others in Africa include:

- ❏ an abundance of natural resources;
- ❏ the dispossession of the black and Afrikaner peasantries;
- ❏ the imposition of a freehold land tenure system;
- ❏ the transformation of the peasantry into wage labourers;
- ❏ the importation of foreign capital and skills;
- ❏ investment in the health, education and general welfare of about 10 per cent of the population;
- ❏ investment in a transportation and communications infrastructure;
- ❏ investment in agriculture, manufacturing and financial services;
- ❏ the establishment of rule-of-law institutions; and
- ❏ the establishment of an independent mass media.

For nearly 140 years, since South Africa's mining industry began in the 1860s with the discovery of diamonds, the country had followed a problematic economic development model.

Its industrialisation was based on the importation of foreign technology and foreign capital, commonly referred to as foreign direct investment. This was how the country's mining, manufacturing and even financial services industries developed until the 1980s, when Western banks and several multinational corporations disinvested from South Africa.

The problem with this model was that it functioned smoothly only when there was a plentiful supply of minerals and other natural resources and, equally importantly, when there was a plentiful supply of relatively cheap, low-skilled labour sitting outside the modern economy and which could be drawn upon with relative ease.

But what happens when the cheap labour supplies dry up because of unionisation and when the plentiful supply of minerals also starts to dry up or becomes more difficult to mine, as has happened to the country's gold deposits, which have become deeper and more inaccessible?

What happened was that the Afrikaner elite resorted to the increased use of force against black workers, which led to its undoing.

Black workers had begun to unionise in the early 1970s and, despite massive repression, the union movement continued to grow rapidly, culminating in the formation of the Congress of South African Trade Unions (Cosatu), in 1985. As a result of pressure, the wages of black miners, which had remained almost unchanged for most of the twentieth century, started to increase.

53

The violent repression by the National Party government of black workers who attempted to unionise led to South Africa's major corporations putting pressure on the government to withdraw apartheid policies in the workplace. The resultant establishment of the Wiehahn and Riekert Commissions in the 1970s led to the abolition of job reservation and, eventually, to the disintegration of the National Party as it split into verligte (enlightened) and verkrampte (reactionary) wings.

Ultimately, the realisation that the country could not survive economically without radical change led the government to convene all-inclusive constitutional negotiations in 1990.

The former chairperson of Barlow Rand, Mike Rosholt, in an interview with *Business Day* on 9 April 2009, acknowledged that self-interest was behind the support by business of black unionisation in the 1970s:

> It was a conscious thing by us [at Barlow Rand]. You need to have a union otherwise you can have a situation where the workers are constantly on strike, but, besides the commercial side of things, a country has to have participation from all its people ... This complete split [between black and white during the apartheid years] couldn't go on forever.[2]

The emergence of the black middle class

The origins of the black middle class date back to the 1830s when the British eventually realised they could not crush the Xhosa without forming alliances with other African tribes. During the war of 1835–37 the British identified three groups as potential allies.

The first group was the amaMfengu or Fingoes;[3] the second was sections of the Xhosa who had become displaced in the succession conflict between Ndlambe and Ngqika,[4] especially the Gqunukwebe clan; and the third was a community of Khoi people living along the valley of the Kat River.

These groups became military allies of the British in their struggle to subdue the Xhosa. In return for their military support the British shared the captured land and cattle with them, as well as with the Afrikaner farmers and with the British 1820 settlers who had formed commandoes to support the British army against the Xhosa. The British introduced their black allies to the ways of the modern capitalist world of the time. They transformed them into peasant farmers and acquainted them with Western religion, writing, modern medicine, Western clothing, modern citizenship and electoral politics. This model was transferred to Natal in the 1840s when the British evicted the Trekboers and took over Natal south of the Tugela River.

Out of this peasantry emerged South Africa's African middle class – Christian, missionary educated, Anglophile, liberal, pro-capitalist and attuned to parliamentary democracy, which was introduced by the British in the Cape Colony in the 1850s.

The African middle class was soon joined, in particular, by the freed Malay and other slaves, many of whom became independent entrepreneurs after the abolition of slavery in 1834–38. During the last quarter of the nineteenth century the former peasant and former slave middle class was joined by free Indians who had paid their way to South Africa and worked as independent merchants, teachers and doctors. The most famous of these was Cambridge-educated lawyer Mohandas Gandhi.

In the 100 years after the enactment of the Glen Grey Act[5] in 1894 the black (including the so-called coloured and Indian) population began to lose its franchise, only regaining it in 1994, when it became the dominant political power in the country. During these 100 years the qualification for the franchise, which, in any event only existed in the Cape and Natal, was repeatedly raised and was eventually removed entirely.

Blacks could not vote in the first national elections after the formation of the Union of South Africa in 1910 and black rights to property ownership were whittled away, while, in terms of the job reservation laws, they were excluded from most skilled work. Despite these strictures, a black middle class began to evolve, through the churches, the professions and through non-governmental organisations, and remained the torchbearer of democracy in South Africa for 100 years while its nineteenth-century partners, the British imperialists, had swapped democracy for super profits from diamonds and gold.

In 1994, it emerged as a powerful black elite that controlled significant institutions, such as the South African Council of Churches and the Catholics Bishops Conference. It provided political leadership to the formidable trade union movements of Cosatu and the National Congress of Trade Unions (Nactu). It was thus seen at home and abroad – by South African big business, by foreign investors and by the British and Americans – as the natural replacement for the floundering Afrikaner elite that had ruled the country since 1907, although, unlike that elite, it still had very little economic power.

Characteristics of the black elite

Liberalism
While the British army was conquering the world, different sections of British society were doing other things. They were fighting against slavery; they were fighting against the

dispossession and mistreatment of defeated communities; they were converting indigenous people to Christianity; they were selling British-manufactured goods to the four corners of the world; and they were promoting the British ideology of liberalism.

The first ideology of the black elite as it emerged in the mid-nineteenth century was, thus, British liberalism, which promoted the sanctity of private property, freedom of speech and association and elected representative government.

African nationalism

Imposed on this essentially Anglophile liberal core ideology was African nationalism, which arose initially in response to attempts by mining companies to dispossess African peasants in order to drive them to the diamond and gold mines as cheap, unskilled manual labour.

It was also an element of the struggle of African priests in the late nineteenth century to take control of missionary churches from white missionaries, a struggle that led the priests to appeal for help from the black American churches, especially the African Methodist Episcopal (AME) Church, which brought with it the 'Africa for the Africans' slogan. It also brought the view, propagated at the time by former slave turned teacher, Booker T. Washington, that black people should 'lift themselves up by their bootstraps'.[6]

African nationalism in South Africa thus dovetailed with liberalism in that it also promoted individual entrepreneurship.

This was how Macah Kunene, a prominent African businessman in Natal, explained the relationship between the black elite and British imperialism when asked by the South African Native Affairs Commission in 1903 if he would like to see the British leave South Africa and return home.

> If the white people and the King [of England] were to desert us now and leave us here, there is a great section of us who have approximated to a great extent to the white man's way of living, and to the white man's way of doing things; and there is a large number of us who have not advanced at all, who have remained as they were practically in former days. I am afraid that those who have remained in their former state would kill us all, particularly civilised Natives, because we have bought lands, they do not approve of the ownership of land. They know too that whenever there has been a war, against Natives like ourselves, we have always been with the (colonial) Government and gone out to assist them in those wars ... Therefore, we feel that we are far better under our (colonial) Government, and are far better than if we were deserted and left to the mercies of our people.[7]

Social democracy

South Africa's black elite entered the twentieth century with liberalism and nationalism as the key components of its ideology.

The Natal Indian Congress was established in 1896 by Gandhi; the African People's Organisation – for coloureds, many of them descendants of slaves – was formed in 1904 by Edinburgh University medical graduate Dr A. Abdurahman; and the African National Congress (ANC), for Africans, was established in 1912 by Columbia University law graduate Pixley ka Isaka Seme.

Social democracy entered the world of the black elite only in the second half of the twentieth century through the influence of the South African Communist Party, whose members played an active role in formulating the ANC's programme, the Freedom Charter, adopted in 1955. Other influences on the black elite immediately after the Second World War included the Soviet and Chinese communist parties and social democratic parties in Western Europe.

The social democracy of the black elite was, however, not influenced by the doctrines of socialism. Rather, it was based on statist economic models which its creators saw as a way of breaking the power of white-owned corporations, thus creating the possibility of the black elite entering business.

Nelson Mandela explained the nationalisation clause

of the Freedom Charter in an article published in 1956 as follows:

> The charter strikes a fatal blow at the financial and gold mining monopolies that have for centuries plundered the country and condemned its people to servitude. The breaking up and democratisation of these monopolies will open up fresh fields for the development of a prosperous non-European bourgeois class. For the first time in the history of this country the non-European bourgeoisie will have the opportunity to own, in their own name and right, mills and factories, and trade and private enterprise will boom and flourish as never before.[8]

* * *

Black Economic Empowerment (BEE) has not, however, proved to be the fatal blow to South Africa's oligarchs that Nelson Mandela and black nationalists of his era once envisioned. In fact, it strikes a fatal blow against the emergence of black entrepreneurship by creating a small class of unproductive but wealthy black crony capitalists made up of ANC politicians, some retired and others not, who have become strong allies of the economic oligarchy that is, ironically, the caretaker of South Africa's de-industrialisation.

CHAPTER 3

THE DE-INDUSTRIALISATION OF SOUTH AFRICA

TWO FEATURES DISTINGUISH SOUTH AFRICA FROM THE REST OF SUB-Saharan Africa. Firstly, it does not have a peasant social class.[1] And secondly, its modern manufacturing and mining private sector is owned mainly by South African citizens, one of the unintended consequences of sanctions and disinvestment in the 1970s and 1980s. These two features have enormous implications for governance as well as for the policy choices available.

While South Africa today is ruled by a political elite with much the same roots and characteristics as most of those in the rest of sub-Saharan Africa, it has little room for manoeuvre because it does not have a passive peasantry to exploit. Instead, it is surrounded by a dynamic private sector owned by South African citizens whose rights are constitutionally entrenched and are enforceable by the propertied classes themselves through the franchise, through the judiciary and through the independent mass media, which see themselves as the watchdog over the rights of citizens.

In addition, African nationalists in South Africa were compelled in the struggle against apartheid to enter into alliances with the black urban working class. South Africa's urban working class is existentially the opposite of peasant smallholders in that it is organised into independent social movements, especially trade unions, which articulate and represent its interests. Central to the interests of the black working class and private sector owners are job creation for the former and profit maximisation for the latter. Both these major social and political forces thus have a common interest in promoting economic growth and in minimising the private consumption of the political elite.

This accounts for South Africa's ability – relatively speaking – to grow its economy, while the economies of the rest of sub-Saharan Africa are stymied by the dead weight of political elite consumption.

All this does not mean that the political elite in South Africa will not try to enrich itself at the expense of private-sector producers. Black Economic Empowerment (BEE) in South Africa is, in reality, another attempt to siphon savings from private-sector operators in an environment where there are no peasants and where most of the private sector is locally owned.

The fact that BEE is an uphill battle for South Africa's political elite is the result of the ability of the private sector to resist dispossession. But these are early days. Time will tell who will emerge best from what could be a titanic struggle by the political elite – recently joined by organised labour – to confiscate the wealth of South Africa's current private-sector owners.

An even bigger question, however, is what impact these struggles will have on the growth potential of the South African economy.

Foreign multinational corporations continue to play an important role in the economy, both as old investors and as new investors. The property rights protection enforced by the South African Constitution also protects foreign investors. The sophistication of the South African economy and its extensive entanglement with the global economy means that foreign corporations have independent clout in South Africa in the sense that the economy cannot operate without international licences, patents, copyrights, and so on.

This point was brought home in the negotiations between

South Africa and the American Chamber of Commerce over black shareholding in American information technology companies operating in the country. Not surprisingly, the giants of United States information and communication technology will not be required to accommodate black shareholders if they do not wish to.[2]

What is Black Economic Empowerment?

Most people in South Africa, in Africa, and the rest of the world naively believe that BEE was an invention of South Africa's black nationalists, especially the African National Congress (ANC), which won the first democratic election in April 1994, leading to Nelson Mandela becoming the country's first black president. This could not be further from the truth. BEE was, in fact, invented by South Africa's economic oligarchs, that handful of white businessmen and their families who control the commanding heights of the country's economy, that is, mining and its associated chemical and engineering industries and finance.

The flagship BEE company, New Africa Investments Limited (Nail), started operating in 1992, two years before the ANC came to power. It was created by the second-largest South African insurance company, Sanlam, with the support of the National Party government-controlled Industrial

Development Corporation (IDC), a state-owned industrial investment bank created in 1940. The formation of Nail was soon followed by the creation of Real African Investment Limited (Rail), sponsored by mining giant Anglo American Corporation through its financial services subsidiary Southern Life.

The object of BEE was to co-opt leaders of the black resistance movement by literally buying them off with what looked like a transfer to them of massive assets at no cost. To the oligarchs, of course, these assets were small change.

Sanlam created Nail by transferring control of one of its small subsidiaries, Metropolitan Life, 85 per cent of whose policy-holders were black, to several ANC and Pan Africanist Congress affiliated leaders. The device used was to split shares of MetLife into a small package, dubbed high-voting shares, which gave the politicians (funded by a loan from the IDC) control of the company. Overnight the politicians were transformed into multi-millionaires without having had to lift a finger because all the financial wizardry was performed by Sanlam's senior executives. All the politicians had to do was show up at the party to launch Nail and thank their benefactor. Even the debt the politicians incurred was largely fictitious as it was MetLife that had to pay it back to the IDC.

This financial razzmatazz was designed to achieve a number of objectives. It was intended to:

❏ wean the ANC from radical economic ambitions, such as nationalising the major elements of the South African economy, by putting cash in the politicians' private pockets, packaged to look like atonement for the sins of apartheid, that is, reparations to black people in general;

❏ provide the oligarchs with prominent and influential seats at the high table of the ANC government's economic policy formulation system;

❏ allow those oligarchs who wanted to shift their company's primary listings and headquarters from Johannesburg to London to do so;

❏ give the oligarchs and their companies the first bite at government contracts that interested them; and

❏ protect the oligarchs from foreign competition while opening up the rest of the economy, especially the consumer goods and manufacturing sector, to the chill winds of international competition.

All these machinations were eventually incorporated into South Africa's democratic Constitution by the creation of a category of citizens, apparently 91 per cent of the population, to be known as Previously Disadvantaged Individuals (PDIs). The ingenious legal notion of previously disadvantaged individuals created the impression that all black South Africans could or would benefit from BEE. This legitimised the co-option payment to the black political elite by dangling before the black masses the possibility that one day they, too, would receive reparations for the wrongs done to them during the apartheid era.

BEE and its subsidiaries – affirmative action and affirmative procurement – which started off as defensive instruments created by the economic oligarchs to protect their assets, have metamorphosed. They have become both the core ideology of the black political elite and, simultaneously, the driving material and enrichment agenda which is to be achieved by maximising the proceeds of reparations that accrue to the political elite. As we shall see below, this has proved to be disastrous for the country.

Reparations

The black elite, which describes itself as made up of PDIs, sees its primary mission as extracting reparations from those who put it in a disadvantaged position. To achieve this requires the transfer of resources from the wrongdoer – perceived to be white-owned businesses and the South African state – to the victim, the PDIs. By this logic the South African state owes the PDIs high-paying jobs. This transfer of wealth from the strong to the weak is what has come to be known as BEE.

Enormous consequences follow from this apparently simple formulation:

1. In order for the wrongdoer to be able to pay reparations, the wrongdoer has to maintain a privileged position. This is the principle of fattening the goose that lays the golden egg. What this means is that the corporations that were allegedly responsible for victimising the PDIs must not be transformed beyond putting a few black individuals in their upper echelons. The protection of these corporations has gone so far as to allow them to move their head offices and primary listings from Johannesburg to London in order to shield them from possible economic and political upheaval in South Africa. At a broader level, the battery of Washington Consensus policies – which include trade liberalisation, balanced budgets, privatisation, inflation targeting, as well as the small state – all serve to protect the interests of South Africa's big business, one of the two main payers of reparations.

2. For the victim to continue to draw reparations it is critical that he or she remains perceived as a victim and as weak. This means that the former freedom fighter must be transformed from a hero who liberated South Africa into an underling. The payment of reparations to the black elite thus achieves the opposite of what it is claimed it was designed to do, that is, make its members leading players in the economy. In reality, it makes members of

the black elite perpetual junior support players to white-controlled corporations.

3. One of the most destructive consequences of the reparations ideology is the black elite's relationship with, and attitude to, the South African state. As the state is said to have been party to the disadvantaging of the PDIs it is therefore also perceived to owe them something. By way of reparations the state must therefore provide PDIs with high-paying jobs. By extension, the assets of the state are seen as fair game. The approach of the black elite to the state is, therefore, not that of using the state to serve the needs of the people but rather of using it, in the first instance, to advance the material interest of PDIs. Not surprisingly, corruption under the ANC government has grown by leaps and bounds, leading Transparency International – the worldwide watchdog on corruption – to downgrade South Africa in the world's corruption tables. According to the Transparency International Corruption Perceptions Index South Africa dropped from number 34 in 2000 to number 54 in 2008. In 2008 the least corrupt countries were Denmark, New Zealand and Sweden and the most corrupt country was Somalia, ranked at 180.[3] Ironically, one of the most important restraining influences on the abuse of the state for the self-enrichment of the black elite is the white-controlled

71

corporations – the abovementioned layers of golden eggs – because these corporations need the South African state to function efficiently in order to provide a stable business environment as well as functioning transport and communication infrastructure. The judiciary and the independent mass media also play an important role in this regard.

4. The ideology of reparations traps members of the black elite into seeing themselves as the beneficiaries of the production of other social groups and therefore primarily as consumers. To facilitate their role as consumers the black elite sees the state essentially as distributive rather than developmental. Most importantly, the black elite don't see themselves as producers and therefore do not envisage themselves as entrepreneurs who can initiate and manage new enterprises. At best, they see themselves as joining existing enterprises, the process of which is to be facilitated by the distributive state through reparations-inspired legislation. This is the most striking difference between the black elite of South Africa and the elites of Asia, where the driving ideology is entrepreneurship.

Through these processes the erstwhile wrongdoer becomes the role model looked up to by the rest of society, including by the PDIs. Consequently, the lifestyle and standard of living of old white South Africa has become the goal to which the new black elite aspires. The reality, however, is that this standard of living can only lead the country to ruin.

The role of the post-apartheid elite

Karl Marx observed that in any given epoch the dominant ideas in a particular society are the ideas of that society's dominant class or classes.[4] Consequently, in order to answer the question 'what constitutes transformation in South Africa today?', I must first answer the question 'who is the dominant class or classes in the country?'

As we have seen, South Africa does not have one dominant class; it has two. The black upper middle class dominates the country's political life today but it plays next to no role in the ownership and control of the productive economy of South Africa; its key role is overseeing the redistribution of wealth towards consumption. It manages (or should that be mismanages?) a few state-owned enterprises inherited from the National Party era.

At the level of the productive economy South Africa has another dominant class, which I call the economic oligarchy. These are the owners and controllers of the Minerals-Energy Complex (MEC), which, according to Ben Fine and Zavareh Rustomjee, constitutes the dominant core of the South

African economy. The MEC includes the financial sector, which, Fine and Rustomjee show, is enmeshed with the country's mining companies.[5]

South Africa, therefore, has a ruling class – the partnership between the politically dominant black upper middle class on the one hand and the economic oligarchy that owns the MEC on the other. This partnership was first identified by Sampie Terreblanche, who pointed out that in the early 1990s two negotiation forums led to the country's new democratic order. The first – the Convention for a Democratic South Africa (Codesa) – he said, consisted of the public negotiations between political parties for the new democratic Constitution. The second, Codesa II, was what he called secret negotiations between the economic oligarchy and representatives of the black upper middle class.[6]

Codesa I and Codesa II gave us South Africa's transformation equation. According to this equation:

Parliamentary Democracy + Globalisation + BEE = Transformation

It is the new ruling class that, in the final analysis, determines what constitutes transformation in South Africa. More accurately, it is this ruling class that determines what is and is not desirable transformation in our society.

Two groups are conspicuously absent from this description

74

of South Africa's ruling class, but are very visible in civil society. These are, on the one hand, the broader capitalist classes, engaged in manufacturing and distribution and, on the other hand, organised labour. The Congress of South African Trade Unions (Cosatu) has made strenuous efforts to play a role in shaping the design of South Africa's economic and social policies, but since 1994 its impact has been largely marginal.

An examination of South Africa's economic and social policies shows that the interests of manufacturers and organised labour come a distant third and fourth – and in some cases don't feature at all – to those of the two dominant classes referred to above.

How does the economic oligarchy see transformation? What does it want transformed (and not transformed)? Similarly, how does the black upper middle class see transformation and what does it want transformed (and not transformed)?

To answer these questions it is necessary to explore the nature of the MEC.

The Minerals-Energy Complex

South Africa is well endowed with natural resources, especially minerals and metals. This has created a unique

South African form of capitalism. The South African economy is dominated by the extraction of minerals from the ground, processing them into metals through the use of electric power and chemicals and selling them to the rest of the world. Most of the assets of the economy are devoted to these activities, which also account for most of the country's exports.

As Fine and Rustomjee see it:

In identifying the MEC as lying at the core of the economy, there is at its own core those sectors associated with minerals and energy in the narrow technical sense. The role of gold as a key sector in the South African economy is well known. Its importance has declined in recent years with the declining price of gold, the fertility of reserves and the emergence of other sources of supply in the world market. However, other metals have gained in prominence, especially platinums. The same is true of coal: it is responsible for 80 per cent of the country's primary energy needs. It also provides for 20 per cent of the country's exports and one-third of all non-gold exports. But very little coal is used for direct energy needs. The vast majority is either converted into electricity (over 50 per cent) or into oil (over 30 per cent). On a global scale, the South African economy is uniquely dependent on electricity and is uniquely electricity-intensive, with levels of consumption per capita comparable, for example, to those of the UK, despite limited domestic consumption by the majority of the population.[7]

Among the industries that constitute the MEC are:

❏ coal, gold, diamond, platinum and other mines;
❏ electricity generation and distribution;
❏ non-metallic mineral products;
❏ iron and steel basic industries;
❏ non-ferrous metals basic industries; and
❏ fertilisers, pesticides, synthetic resins, plastics, basic chemicals and petroleum.

Of course, minerals have been a blessing for South Africa (and, indeed, for Africa) in that they have helped to kick-start a process of capital accumulation by attracting foreign investors and promoting the construction of physical infra-structure. Among the weaknesses of the MEC, however, is its dependence on wasting non-renewable assets, dependence on imported technology and capital, and overexposure to volatile world markets. Most importantly, however, a key characteristic of the MEC is its dependence on abundant, cheap, unskilled labour.

The transformation equation

The primary object of the economic oligarchy during the Codesa II negotiations was to ensure the preservation of the MEC. The quid pro quo for representatives of the black upper middle class, the ANC politicians, who agreed to the preservation of the MEC was the creation of BEE.

The second object of the economic oligarchy was to persuade the emerging black political elite to agree to the use of globalisation to maintain the system of cheap labour required by the MEC. In the past, cheap labour for the MEC was achieved, among other methods, by recruiting unskilled labour from the vast region of southern Africa as far north as Angola and Tanganyika. Long before the Southern African Development Community (SADC) was formed, in the 1980s, southern Africa, as an integrated region, was invented by Wenela, the Chamber of Mines's Witwatersrand Native Labour Association.

The old ways of maintaining cheap labour, detailed by Francis Wilson in *Labour in the South African Gold Mines*,[8] could not be sustained after southern African countries gained independence and once trade unionism grew among black workers in South Africa. The new way of keeping labour cheap was therefore to import wage goods from cheaper producers in the global economy, especially China.

There are several ways of keeping down the costs of labour, the use of brute force being one, but, as we have seen, it is not a method that is sustainable in the long term. A far more effective method is to keep down the cost of the products the working class consumes.

In South Africa there is a growing tendency to import these products from cheaper producers. One of the most obvious areas in which this tendency is evident – to the detriment of workers who lose their jobs – is in the clothing, textile and footwear industry, where local products are increasingly being replaced by cheap imports, especially from East, South-East and South Asia. The supply of food, too, is affected, with cheaper products coming in from Argentina and South-East Asia. Other products consumed by the working class are increasingly imported, among them textbooks, furniture, cooking utensils, white goods (large domestic appliances) and television sets.

The outcome of the use of globalisation to provide cheap consumer goods for the working class in the MEC has resulted in the destruction of the non-MEC manufacturing sector. This explains why capitalists in that sector were excluded from the Codesa II deliberations. It also explains the exclusion of organised labour. The destruction of the manufacturing sector is at the root of the growing impoverishment of

South Africans, leading, as it does, to increasing structural unemployment.

* * *

We have seen in Chapter 2 that the black middle class promoted parliamentary democracy in South Africa for more than 100 years. It was also the avowed enemy of the MEC, which it saw, quite rightly, as being behind the dispossession of the African peasants, the introduction of the pass laws, the perpetuation of the system of cheap labour and the exclusion of blacks from property ownership.

The nationalisation of the MEC was therefore at the top of the list for the black middle class. Ironically, nationalisation of the mines had also, at one stage, been at the top of the list for the Afrikaner elite under the leadership of the National Party. As stated above, BEE was the bribe offered by the economic oligarchy at Codesa II to the black middle class for it to drop its demand for nationalisation.

What should be clear is that while the transformation equation has brought political stability and elements of prosperity, in the longer term, by undermining the country's manufacturing industries and bringing about the decline in private manufacturing sector employment since the late 1980s, it is creating a vast urban underclass.

Although, as is clear from this exposition, not all ruling classes are the same (because different social and economic systems spawn different relationships between the dominant classes and the dominated or subordinate classes), ruling classes all over the world, and throughout history, have used their dominant position in society to protect and advance their interests. In this regard present-day South Africa is no different.

Karl Marx observed:

> In the social production of their existence, men inevitably enter into definite relations, which are independent of their will, namely relations of production appropriate to a given stage in the development of their material forces of production. The totality of these relations of production constitutes the economic structure of society, the real foundation, on which arises a legal and political superstructure and to which correspond definite forms of social consciousness. The mode of production of material life conditions the general process of social, political and intellectual life.[9]

South Africa's social and economic structure is dominated by the MEC, which has led to a uniquely South African system of capitalism that is mining, cheap labour and electricity intensive. On top of this structure sits an economic oligarchy that, with its army of managers, controls a handful of large companies. These companies in turn control large mineral reserves, which, in some instances, exist only, or mainly, in South Africa – platinum being a case in point.

In the 120 years since the discovery of gold in the 1880s South Africa's economic oligarchy has ridden out many storms. It organised an armed insurrection against the Paul Kruger government in conjunction with the Jameson Raid (1895–96), instigated the war between the British and the Boers in 1899, and saw off insurrections and strikes by both white and black workers in 1907, 1911, 1913, 1922, 1946 and 1987.

Most importantly, it has kept the MEC intact through various nationalist governments – both Afrikaner and black – which were hostile to the central role and activities of the MEC in South Africa's economic life. Over the years the economic oligarchy perfected ways of placating successive political elites, BEE being the latest of these methods.

The power of the oligarchy to damage the political elite in a confrontation was brought into sharp focus when it leaked out that the ANC government contemplated using the BEE device to take control of the MEC. The economic oligarchy, using its immense international networks, sounded alarm bells in global financial capitals. Within hours, huge chunks of South Africa's wealth vanished.

South Africa's transformation formula is thus not merely

based on a common economic vision within the ruling class; it is underwritten by the independent ability of each constituent portion of the ruling class to defend its interests.

The political elite, of course, has the wherewithal to damage the interests of the economic oligarchy by using the state, which it controls through democratic processes. The reality, however, is that the political elite is comparatively more vulnerable since the economic oligarchy can promote new political parties to challenge a hostile ruling party.

But skirmishes within the ruling class pale in comparison to the challenges posed by South Africa's shrinking manufacturing industries. We have seen that the formula 'Transformation = Parliamentary Democracy + Globalisation + BEE' leads, inevitably, to opening up the economy to the chill winds of Asian competition.

The MEC is immune to global competition as it sells minerals and metals that are largely unique to South Africa. Manufacturing industries do not have such natural protection, however. After 1990 employment in South Africa's private sector declined steadily, fuelling the growing impoverishment of many South Africans. At the same time, the top 10–20 per cent of the population became even richer, benefiting from BEE wealth redistribution programmes and, until recently, also from steeply increasing commodity prices.

Placating the poor

South Africa is able to undertake both BEE and large-scale social welfare expenditure because of its vast natural resources, which are now selling at a premium thanks to the rapid industrialisation of the large countries of Asia. South Africa's fabulous mineral wealth has been seen as a blessing since the discovery of diamonds and gold in the nineteenth century. What has been overlooked is the curse that goes with such wealth.

Since the current commodities boom began in the late 1990s the ANC government has ratcheted up public spending on welfare. Why? Out of the goodness of its heart, reply the ANC leaders. Not so, say the doubters; it has been done to placate the poor so that they do not rebel and, most importantly, it has been done to buy the vote of the poor.

In his address to the ANC's watershed Polokwane conference in December 2007 President Thabo Mbeki went to great lengths to explain the many good things the ANC government has done for South Africa's poor. He said the number of South Africans living below the poverty line had fallen from 51.4 per cent in 2001 to 43.2 per cent in 2006, and that the number of people receiving social grants had increased from 2 587 373 in 1999 to more than 12 million in 2006.

84

Are South Africa's poor happy and grateful to the ANC government? In theory they should be, given the largesse they are receiving, but there are many signs that they are far from happy. At times they bite the very hand that feeds them. This is where the so-called resource curse comes in.

A country develops when it is able to harness the energies of its people and put them to productive use. There are, of course, one or two exceptions to this rule. For example, at the height of its power the Roman Empire sustained a large population in Rome by feeding it on the spoils of conquest. The result was that the populace had no need to be productive; they received free food from the state and were entertained by gladiators.

In today's world the ways of Ancient Rome are not an option, quite simply because modern states, even the smallest of them, have the capacity to resist plunder from even the most powerful. The next best thing to living off the wealth of other people's land, as the Roman masses did, is living off the fat of one's own land. This is what happens in resource-rich countries.

Oil-producing countries are today the best illustration of how to live off the fat of the land. With very little effort they pump crude oil out of the ground and sell it to foreigners for fabulous prices. In most cases the citizens of oil-producing countries play a minimum role in pumping up the oil – this is frequently done by foreigners, who have the skills and technology to do so. The local people, who become mere spectators to this process, benefit from the royalties foreign oil companies pay to the governments of oil-producing countries. These governments, in turn, distribute these revenues to their citizens for their private consumption.

The situation in South Africa is similar to that in oil-producing countries in that it, too, has natural resources that are valuable to foreigners, who are willing to pay top dollar for them. While it takes more people to dig out South Africa's minerals than it takes to pump crude oil, mining is still a small employer. Despite this, it makes a massive contribution to the country's wealth in that it accounts for more than half of export earnings.

The value that the few people employed in mining produce far exceeds their income. Government, therefore, derives large revenues from mining activity, which it can redistribute to the rest of society, who do not work on the mines. In other words, it is possible for a large number of people in South Africa not to work but to live off state revenues redistributed from mining activities. The higher the price foreigners pay for our minerals, the larger the number of people who can be sustained by government social grants without working. This is what is called a resource curse; governments of resource-rich countries work on the assumption that their people need not work and will be happy to live off social grants.

This is precisely the trap into which the ANC government has fallen. At least a quarter of the population receives social grants that would not be available if South Africa were not rich in minerals. Without mineral wealth to redistribute government would have to work harder and be more creative about finding solutions to unemployment and poverty. Resource wealth makes it possible for the government not to have to put an effort into redeveloping the economy to create more jobs.

But do social grants make people happy, as the ANC government expects? Evidently they do not. Ironically, while they contribute to putting some food on the table, at a broader level they make the recipients more insecure because they fear the government might withdraw or reduce the size of the grants.

Grants also add to and/or accentuate the humiliation that unemployed people feel about being dependent and unproductive and therefore unable to look after themselves and their families. Each time they collect their grants recipients are subjected to all manner of humiliation from the government officials who administer these grants. In addition, they are stigmatised by the rest of society as being idle, worthless and parasitic.

So, what do South Africa's subsidised and marginalised

people do to regain their self-respect? They support dema-gogues who claim they, too, are marginalised and therefore want to replace the ruling elites with people-friendly gov-ernments. This, in a nutshell, is what happened at the ANC conference in December 2007, when delegates voted out their president and most of his cabinet.

Jacob Zuma, with the support of Cosatu, the South African Communist Party and the ANC Youth League, ran a campaign telling ANC members, most of whom are poor, that he, Zuma, like them, is despised and marginalised by the elite who run the ANC and its government. This is the case, the story went, because he is a mere peasant, like most ANC and Cosatu members. Zuma argued that there was a conspiracy by the elite to ensure that he, and poor people like him, were kept from power and would therefore not benefit from the victory over apartheid.

Zuma's message resonated with many trade unionists, among them Cosatu General Secretary Zwelinzima Vavi, who grew up as a farm labourer and worked his way to a position of power by fighting against discrimination and humiliation under apartheid. Cosatu leaders and members feel especially marginalised because the cabinet takes major decisions about the economy without so much as informing them.

These are the dynamics that make South Africa a slowly and quietly ticking time bomb. The country's mode of entry into the world economy was negotiated to meet the demands of the MEC for cheap consumer goods, without taking into account the ability of the country's manufacturing industries to survive, compete and continue to create jobs. South Africa, therefore, needs a new transformation equation. This cannot be developed without the active participation of manufacturing and distribution sector capitalists, organised labour, academics and other civil society players. Achieving this goal clearly entails broadening South Africa's ruling class to include classes of society that are currently excluded.

The wrong model of development

The high standard of living of the majority of whites in South Africa was achieved by the creation of an artificial scarcity of skilled manual labour and professionals. This was the purpose of job reservation, which was in place for most of the twentieth century.

For South Africa to develop it needs to do the opposite – to create an overabundance of artisans, technicians, professionals and managers, the formula that has led to the rapid development of China and India.

An abundant supply of skills will serve the most important purpose of driving down labour costs, especially those of the supervisory, managerial, technical and professional classes.

This can be achieved in a number of ways:

❏ In the short term it can be achieved by importing skilled people from the rest of the world. This was the method the United States used to develop Silicon Valley – it imported a large number of information technology specialists from India.

❏ In the longer term it can only be achieved by a massive educational drive that actually produces qualified people, especially scientists and engineers.

❏ In the medium term it could be achieved by a combination of both training and the importation of skills.

The high price of skilled categories of labour at present is the reason for the massive social inequality in South Africa. Affirmative action laws, which are embedded in BEE scorecards, do for black professionals and the black middle class in general what job reservation did for whites – force up their salaries by creating scarcity, and thereby de-link remuneration from productivity. Not surprisingly we are now seeing the greatest inequality in South Africa among Africans, who have the lowest number of qualified professionals.

The real problem is that high unit labour costs in South Africa are the result of the manipulation of skilled and professional labour categories – by the white elite in the past and by the black elite today. The reason why South African manufacturing industries are unable to compete against those in China, India, Vietnam and Indonesia, is not that labourers in Asia are paid slave-labour wages – in fact, wages there do not differ materially from those paid in South Africa. It is also not the economies of scale resulting from the vast populations of those countries. Rather, it is that South Africa has encouraged the development of bloated middle and senior levels of management that are vastly overpaid.

The right model of development

The model described above is not sustainable. In the past South Africa did not have to compete with other Third World countries because it produced unique minerals, which were only sold to developed Western countries.

Immediately after the Second World War the South African manufacturing sector was able to grow because labour costs, especially those of unskilled black labour, were very low in relation to unskilled labour costs in developed countries, which were the only competitors to South Africa's manufacturing sector.

But the world economy has changed entirely from what it was between 1945 and 1978, when China adopted an open-door economic policy. South Africa's competitors are no longer the high labour cost Western countries but the low labour cost Asian countries, which have made enormous investments in the education and health of their populations. Asian unskilled labour is, in general, more productive than that of South Africa because it is better educated, and Asian skilled and professional labour is cheaper because it is abundant.

One way of competing against China would be to follow the South Korean course of moving into increasingly higher tech industries, but this option is not open to South Africa because of the country's low skills profile.

The second way would be to do exactly what China is doing – invest heavily in the health and skills of the population and thereby eliminate the artificial shortage of skilled labour that drives costs up. For example, China produces 600 000 new engineers every year, nine times as many as the United States.[10]

For the emerging new black elite the message should be clear. If South Africa is to develop in the twenty-first century and rid itself of endemic poverty and high unemployment the elite in this country cannot continue to enjoy the standards of living of the middle classes of the West without the equivalent productivity. The ANC is caught in a quandary. On the one hand, its members and leaders want to preserve, largely intact, the economic system inherited from the National Party era so they can benefit from it. On the other hand, they hanker for change that will ameliorate the growing inequalities and pauperisation among blacks.

The solution to the potential crises caused by the ANC's dilemma can only come from the emergence of a leadership, within or outside the ANC, with meaningful policies for building a more inclusive society in South Africa. BEE, which benefits the black elite, and social welfare programmes, which benefit the poor, do not lead to such social inclusiveness; if anything, they entrench the inequalities inherited from the past and exacerbate new inequalities among the black population.

There is, of course, a second option, which is to go back to being a producer of primary raw materials, which would feed Asia's industrialisation and, at the same time, nurture a small, high-living multiracial elite that lives in an enclave of prosperity.

Liberalism sheds its entrepreneurial component

Western liberalism has proved to be one of the longest-lasting ideologies of the modern world that emerged with the British Industrial Revolution on the one hand and the French Revolution on the other. As already stated, liberalism is made up of many ingredients. It is, however, the drive of entrepreneurship that gives it both its staying power and its dynamism. Liberalism ultimately triumphed over communism, not because of its superior military might – communism more than matched the military prowess of liberalism; rather, it was liberal capitalism's great drive to innovate and thus constantly improve its productivity that communism could not match.

The peaceful demise of communism in central and eastern Europe came about because both the leaders and the mass of the people in those societies arrived at the realisation that communism could not improve their welfare the way liberal capitalism could. A new and interesting development, however, is that China and Vietnam have combined monopoly of power by the Communist Party with entrepreneurship.

In Chapter 2 we discussed how over the centuries the liberalism of the South African black elite became overlaid with African nationalism and later with a statist version of social democracy. However, throughout these transitions liberalism retained, as a cornerstone of its ideology, entrepreneurship for the black elite as well as for the black population at large.

For example, John Dube, the first president of the ANC, founded Ohlange Institute in 1904, modelled on Booker T. Washington's Tuskegee Institute.[11] Dube also established *iLanga lase Natal*, an isiZulu newspaper that survives to this day. First ANC Secretary-General Solomon T. Plaatje was another entrepreneur, starting a publishing firm that published a Setswana newspaper.

What started to happen in the 1980s, however, in conjunction with changes in other parts of the world, was that the liberalism of the black elite began to shed its entrepreneurial component. BEE and various forms of reparations or rent seeking have all but replaced entrepreneurship as the economic component in the liberalism of the country's black elite.

Today, therefore, South Africa has all the trappings of a modern liberal capitalist society – entrenched private property, universal suffrage, freedom of speech and association, regular democratic elections, independent mass media and separation of powers. The one missing factor is support for entrepreneurship from both the politically dominant black elite and the dominant economic elite, who are protected from domestic and foreign competition by the political elite in return for reparations.

The consequences of the disappearance of entrepreneurship as part of the ideology of South Africa's political and economic elites are becoming manifest with every passing day.

South Africa's core economy is shrinking into a minerals

producing and exporting enclave with a core financial and distribution services sector. The country's core manufacturing sector, outside of minerals processing and basic chemicals industries and food processing, is not growing. The rest of the manufacturing sector, which should be the key driver of entrepreneurship and innovation in the economy, is being replaced by ballooning imports, especially from Asia.

In a society where entrepreneurship is considered an unnecessary distraction, and is even discouraged in favour of consumption funded through state redistribution policies, as is the case in South Africa (and indeed, with a few exceptions, in all of Africa), it follows that the general well-being and advancement of the mass of the population becomes problematic. The masses cease to have an influence through their labour on how the society survives and reproduces itself and they thus become marginalised.

In this, the second decade of South Africa's democracy, the country faces numerous challenges that, to a significant extent, are the results of this general marginalisation of a growing proportion of the country's population:

❏ A large and, according to the United Nations, growing number of households are living in poverty – a fact reflected in the decline of South Africa's human development index between 1995 and 2003.[12]

❏ Growing inequality among Africans, with the black elite becoming increasingly rich while the great majority of people, especially in the former homelands, continue to live in poverty.[13]

❏ Rising unemployment coupled with a shrinking manufacturing sector, which in 2008 accounts for only 16 per cent of South Africa's GDP – down from about 25 per cent in 1990 and earlier. In South Korea manufacturing accounts for 35 per cent of GDP and in China it accounts for a massive 51 per cent.

❏ South Africa is facing a huge drop in life expectancy, which, in two years (between 2003 and 2005) declined from 48.4 years to 43.3 years due, in part, to the country's inability to control the HIV/Aids pandemic which is additionally fed by the poverty levels referred to above.[14]

❏ An unproductive education system that sucks in huge amounts of money but produces a large army of dropouts and many who are inappropriately qualified for the South African economy. Despite the massive expenditure on education, which consumes nearly 6 per cent of GDP, South Africa only produced 24 black engineering graduates in 2004.[15]

❏ South Africa continues to be at the bottom of the class in entrepreneurship rankings worldwide.[16]

As stated above, capitalists do not play as central a role in the modern economy as they did between the fifteenth and twentieth centuries because modern capitalist enterprises are managed by professionals who are not, themselves, necessarily capitalists.

Who, then, is the managerial class accountable to since it is no longer accountable to the capitalists? In today's corporate world the reality is that managers are accountable only to other managers. The appointment of non-executive board members represents an attempt to overcome this problem, but this has been largely unsuccessful. The crisis of accountability of the modern management class recently showed itself in the fraudulent accounting of such mega companies as Enron, Parmalat, WorldCom and Arthur Anderson, to name but a few.

In South Africa, this crisis of accountability also applies, with sometimes disastrous consequences, to the state, affecting the mass of the poor black population, whose lives are touched daily by the state through its provision of social grants, community services, and so on.

The South African state is run largely by the black elite, who comprise the professional managers – from politicians to civil servants. There are issues of accountability in the state sector. Public health crises, be it typhoid in Delmas (a small town outside Johannesburg), the theft of medicines from public hospitals or the cholera epidemic inherited from Zimbabwe which raged in several South African provinces in early 2009, are expressions of this accountability crisis, as is the country's rapidly deteriorating education system.

This will only change when state managers are made personally accountable for their actions to the electorate rather than to other politicians, something that is not likely to happen in the foreseeable future, except in the unlikely event that the ANC government accedes to mounting pressure to change the electoral system from the current proportional representation model.

In 2002, the country's then Minister of Home Affairs, Mangosuthu Buthelezi, appointed an Electoral Task Team to undertake a review of the electoral system. The team, chaired by a former leader of the Democratic Party, Dr Frederick van Zyl Slabbert, recommended a mixed-member proportional system whereby South Africa would be broken into con-stituencies with a proportion of members of parliament elected from constituencies, and the remainder from national party lists, to ensure proportionality.

The ANC government rejected the recommendation and shelved the report, but questions of accountability have not gone away. The increasing use of parliament as a tool for implementing the decisions of the ruling party rather than as a vehicle for executing the will of ordinary South

Africans has resulted in a new groundswell of demands for representatives at all levels of government to answer to the electorate rather than to their party bosses.

In January 2009 another report, by a panel of eleven 'eminent persons' commissioned by parliament, again found that the electoral system needed to be changed to make members of parliament more accountable to voters, and that this should be done by means of a system that combined proportional representation and a constituency system – a recommendation which, even if it should be accepted, came too late to affect the 22 April 2009 elections, thus ensuring five more years of party bosses wielding the whip.

Those pressing for the changes that might reverse some of the setbacks of recent years should not hold their breath.

CHAPTER 4

THE MAKING OF A FAILED AFRICAN STATE

IN 1980 ZIMBABWE WAS A PROMISING, ALMOST PROSPEROUS AFRICAN country, well endowed with an array of minerals and a diversified agriculture. But in its 29 years of independence everything that could possibly go wrong has done so – economics, politics, foreign policy, public health ... even the weather – to the detriment of the Zimbabwean people, as shown by the declining per capita Gross Domestic Product (GDP) in Figure 4.1 (on page 102).

Years of economic sanctions imposed by the United Nations and designed to bring the illegal Ian Smith regime to order had led to the development of a fairly sophisticated

Figure 4.1 **Zimbabwe's GDP Growth (1990–2008)**

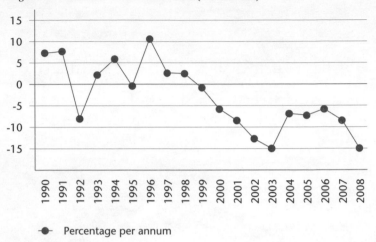

Source: Tony Hawkins, unpublished lectures, 2009.

manufacturing sector and Zimbabwe was well served by a competent financial services sector run by a handful of British banks and insurance companies. The return of well-trained black exiles after independence in April 1980 added to an existing pool of highly skilled and enterprising whites.

Economic decline

Contrary to what has become conventional wisdom, the collapse of the economy is not due solely to mismanagement by Robert Mugabe's Zanu-PF (Zimbabwe African National

Union – Patriotic Front) government. In 1980 Zimbabwe's leading exports included asbestos, gold, ferro-alloys and tobacco. At more than US$800 an ounce then, gold was king.

Since those heady days the picture has changed dramatically. In the 1980s Western countries outlawed asbestos for health reasons. This wiped out a large foreign-exchange earner and deprived many Zimbabweans of well-paying jobs. Then the price of gold began to slide, and dropped steadily over two decades. In 2000 it languished below US$300 an ounce and only in the past few years has it increased again, now reaching more than US$800 an ounce.

Even Zimbabwe's premier cash crop, Virginia tobacco, had an uncertain future because of the growing awareness in rich Western countries of the damage to health caused by smoking. This meant cigarette manufacturers had to sell more of their product to the poorer populations of Asia, Latin America, Africa and Eastern Europe, resulting in a drop in tobacco prices and a drop in tobacco production, as Figure 4.2 (on page 104) illustrates. Interestingly, and perhaps because the Mugabe government had removed from the commercial farms the experienced farmers, farm managers and farm workers who knew how to grow flue-cured Virginia tobacco, the recovery in the price of tobacco in 2006–08 has not seen a corresponding increase in Zimbabwe's production of tobacco.

Figure 4.2 **Zimbabwe's tobacco production (1990–2009)**

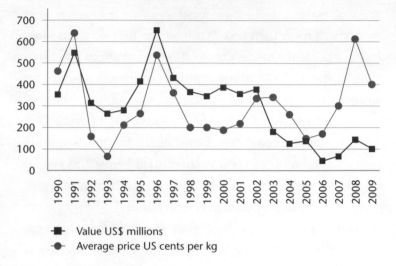

Value US$ millions
Average price US cents per kg

Source: Tony Hawkins, unpublished lectures, 2009.

All was not doom and gloom, though. Independence (in 1980) brought many benefits, among them large amounts of foreign aid, which helped to forestall economic decline. There was even a trickle of private foreign direct investment.

Independence also made it possible for Zimbabwe to become a member of organisations such as the Southern African Development Community (SADC), the Common Market for Eastern and Southern Africa (Comesa), the Lomé Convention and the World Trade Organization, all of which helped to diversify the country's export markets.

104

Over the years Zimbabwe tried to introduce new export products such as platinum, beef and cut flowers. It also expanded exports of sugar, maize, clothing and textiles, as well as steel and steel products.

An achievement for which the Mugabe government deserves due acknowledgement was the introduction among peasants of cotton as a cash crop. This was a painstaking process that required research and the establishment of comprehensive extension services to support the farmers.

However, these efforts did not bridge the growing gap between imports and exports (as illustrated in Figure 4.3),

Figure 4.3 **Zimbabwean trade volumes (1990–2004)**

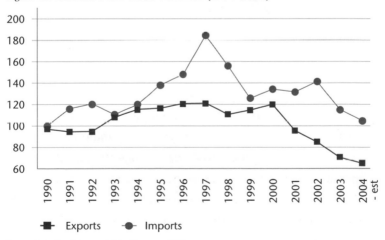

Source: Tony Hawkins, unpublished lectures, 2009.

and therefore the increasing shortage of foreign exchange. The government tried to manage this shortage with devices such as import licences, exchange controls, and the addition of locally distilled alcohol (ethanol) to petrol. But these measures only delayed the day of reckoning. Two things began to happen in the short term.

Firstly, Zimbabwe's foreign debt grew. Secondly, corruption among government officials began to play a prominent role in the distribution of import licences and, later, of scarce imported products. One of these scarce products was cars, which were assembled at Willowvale Motors, a government-owned company. Politicians and government officials jumped the queue, buying at government-controlled prices and selling at open-market prices – in the process making a fortune. The first decade of Zimbabwe's independence thus ended with a huge scandal involving senior government ministers and officials.[1]

In the medium term the growing foreign exchange crunch was leading to a more dangerous economic situation. In the 1990s Zimbabwe found itself unable to maintain, replace and modernise its industrial machinery. Its manufacturing industries thus became increasingly uncompetitive at exactly the time that Africa was opening up to South African exports. South Africa's exports started eating into the Zimbabwean market for manufactured goods, contributing to the decline of Zimbabwe's manufacturing industries as a percentage of GDP, as Figure 4.4 shows.

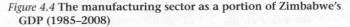

Figure 4.4 **The manufacturing sector as a portion of Zimbabwe's GDP (1985–2008)**

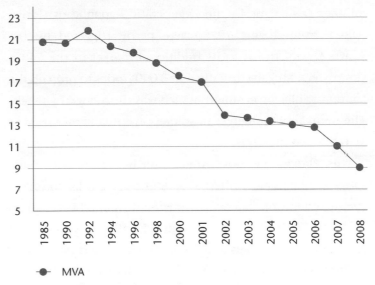

Source: Tony Hawkins, unpublished lectures, 2009.

As if all this were not enough, the International Monetary Fund (IMF) – the godfather of financially strapped nations – was breathing down the Mugabe government's neck, demanding that it lift exchange and import controls.

The inevitable happened. On the one hand, South African products flooded into Zimbabwe; and on the other hand,

Zimbabwean products were being edged out of markets in southern, central and eastern Africa by cheaper and better-quality South African products.

There was a popular belief in Zimbabwe that the country's military campaigns in the Democratic Republic of Congo (DRC), from August 1998, were partly triggered by the South African threat to its traditional market in the DRC's Copperbelt. Mugabe initially sent 3 000 troops to prop up the Laurent Kabila government, which was threatened by rebels. The number of Zimbabwean soldiers eventually increased to 11 000.[2]

This drove the government further into the IMF's suffocating embrace, where it sought help for the country's ever-deteriorating balance of payment. Something had to give. The Zimbabwe dollar nosedived, inflation skyrocketed and black professionals and other skilled workers poured out of Zimbabwe into South Africa, Botswana and the West.

Clearly the people, especially the urban population, had had enough. They voted not only with their feet but with their ballots. In 1995 a Harare constituency elected to parliament Margaret Dongo, a genuine war veteran, who was opposed to Zanu-PF policies.[3]

The role of commercial agriculture

Zimbabwe is a country of enticing myths and legends. A persistent myth, now promising to gain international acceptance, is that white farmers owned most of the best land in the country but, out of malice, they underutilised it, thereby causing untold damage to the economy.[4] If this land were redistributed to black peasant farmers, the myth goes, Zimbabwe would prosper and its people would be saved from their economic and social woes.

This is completely false. In fact, large tracts of land in Zimbabwe are not owned by white farmers but by multinational corporations and the state. It is true that land is underutilised, but this applies to all land, irrespective of who owns it. The reason for this underutilisation is a shortage of capital, a problem that applies to all the country's farmers, be they white commercial farmers or black peasants.

Like all African countries Zimbabwe is not able to generate enough savings to develop its agriculture fully. In order to bring more land under cultivation the country would need to invest hugely in roads, irrigation, research, silos, railways, agricultural machinery, barns, and so on. This investment is needed whether it is white or black farmers who own the land. Since the investment is not forthcoming, large tracts of land are uncultivated in the black peasant areas as well as in white-owned, state-owned and multinational corporation-owned areas.

Anyone who ventures into Zimbabwe's communal areas would be struck by the huge areas of land lying uncultivated and used, instead, as common pasture. If these farmers had the capital they would use tractors, or even mules or horses, to plough the land and use it more productively.

Herein, then, lies the nub of Zimbabwe's land redistribution dilemma. If all the land currently owned by white farmers were tomorrow transferred to black peasant farmers it would make no difference either to the welfare of those black farmers or to Zimbabwe's overall economic performance unless the redistribution was accompanied by a major injection of new capital. Robert Mugabe and his government know this, as does the British government and, quite probably, the peasants themselves.

Since 1980 the Zimbabwean and British governments have worked to try to address the land redistribution issue, which has been a centrepiece of Zanu-PF's political platform since the days of the liberation war.

The Zimbabwe Land Resettlement Programme did not succeed precisely because the government could not come up with its share of the capital required, not only to buy land but also to improve it by building the roads, fences, water and sewerage works, new schools and clinics that were needed if the resettled land was to become productive.

* * *

What makes the tragedy presently playing out in Zimbabwe so devastating is that it was all so predictable – the same had happened in Algeria and Kenya; will Namibia and South Africa be next?

All five of these countries share a number of elements: all were settler colonies and all were liberated after a protracted armed struggle against white minority regimes, achieving varying degrees of independence from their mother countries.

In each country the armed struggle was led by political parties whose leaders, in order to gain the support of the populace, promised great changes – many of which were unrealistic. When independence came the leaders found themselves unable to deliver and started to backtrack.

Where electoral systems survived, as in Zimbabwe, opposition parties held the governing parties to their promises. Zanu-PF has desperately searched for ways to silence the opposition, combining the use of violence against individual supporters of the opposition with new forms of gerrymandering and manipulating voters' rolls.

The Appendix: 'Gukurahundi', which starts on page 177, describes some of the brutal methods used by Zanu-PF to terrorise the people of Zimbabwe.

Zimbabwe's population is divided into approximately three sectors: 30 per cent in urban areas, 20 per cent in commercial farming areas and 50 per cent in peasant farming areas. Most of Zanu-PF's electoral support came from the peasant faming areas, although a significant number of Ndebele-speaking peasants do not support the party. The strategy Zanu-PF adopted was to try to disenfranchise as many of the commercial farming population and the urban population as possible. The dismantling of commercial agriculture and the expulsion of farmers and workers in this sector effectively disenfranchised 20 per cent of the electorate and destroyed the heart of the economy.

In June 2005 the Zanu-PF government embarked on a massive programme to drive parts of the urban population out of the cities in what was called Operation Murambatsvina ('clean out the filth'). The United Nations estimates that this operation, which destroyed the homes of many urban dwellers, affected 2.4 million people, depriving the victims of a home address and, consequently, effectively eliminating them from the voters' roll.

In this way the ruling party contrived to win elections despite its clear lack of popularity.

As the country was to learn to its cost, commercial agriculture did not function in isolation from the rest of the economy; rather, it was its key driver, producing goods whose export earned most of Zimbabwe's hard currency. The agricultural sector also bought manufactured goods from Zimbabwe's secondary industries, thus acting as a market for producers of fertilisers, pesticides, agricultural equipment, and so on.

Besides supplying the country's food needs, commercial farmers produced raw materials or feedstock for manufacturers, for example: cotton, which went into the making of textiles; vegetables and fruit that supplied food processors in the cities; grain that went into the milling industries and further downstream into bread, confectionery, brewing, animal feed, and so on. Commercial agriculture was also closely linked to peasant agriculture, with commercial farmers growing the hybrid seeds that made it possible for Zimbabwe's peasant farmers to become productive, especially in growing white maize, a staple food for the bulk of the populace.

In short, commercial agriculture rather than mining constituted the backbone of the country's economy, not merely because of what it produced but also because of the secondary employment it created in industries such as manufacturing, financial services, transportation and storage, as well as construction and mining. Commercial agriculture was itself the largest employer in Zimbabwe before 2000. Thus, when Zanu-PF in its desperate effort to cling to power, embarked on the process of dismantling commercial agriculture it dug a huge grave in which to bury the country and its people.

The devastating results are evident in the moribund economy, rampant inflation, mass unemployment, decimation of the education and health sectors and in unbridled starvation and the spread of disease, all of which have led to millions abandoning the country for its neighbours.

Origins of the African Renaissance

In 1997 South Africa's then deputy president, Thabo Mbeki, attracted the world's attention when he announced the arrival of the African Renaissance:

> Those who have eyes to see, let them see. The African Renaissance is upon us. As we peer through the looking glass darkly, this may not be obvious. But it is upon us.
>
> What we have been talking about is the establishment of genuine and stable democracies in Africa, in which the systems of governance will flourish because they derive their authority and legitimacy from the will of the people.

The point must be made that the new political order owes its existence to the African experience of many decades which teaches us, as Africans, that what we tried did not work, that the one-party states and the military governments will not work ...

There exists within our continent a generation which has been victim to all the things which created this negative past. This generation remains African and carries with it an historic pride which compels it to seek a place for Africans equal to all the other peoples of our common universe.

It knows and is resolved that, to attain that objective, it must resist all tyranny, oppose all attempts to deny liberty by resort to demagogy, repulse the temptation to describe African life as the ability to live on charity, engage the fight to secure the emancipation of the African woman, and reassert the fundamental concept that we are our own liberators from oppression, from underdevelopment and poverty, from the perpetuation of an experience from slavery, to colonisation, to apartheid, to dependence on alms.

It is this generation whose sense of rage guarantees Africa's advance towards its renaissance.

This is an Africa which is already confronting the enormous challenge of uprooting corruption in African life. The insistence on such notions as transparency and accountability addresses, in part, this vexed question.

On this, as on other questions on which the continent succeeded, however difficult they may have seemed, we are convinced that victory is certain ...

As all other peoples, ours demand a better life. This requires of our governments, the private sector and non-governmental organisations that they continue to work ceaselessly towards meeting people's basic needs in jobs, welfare, education, health, the alleviation of poverty and so on.

Reforms that seek to undermine the continent's medium and longer term ability to discharge its responsibility to its peoples in these areas on a sustained basis will lead to frustration and renewed social turmoil ...[5]

But when the much-heralded renaissance actually arrived in Zimbabwe three years later, in February 2000 in the form of a new political party, and threatened the power of Zanu-PF, southern Africa's leaders took fright and became paralysed as President Robert Mugabe set out to extinguish it by force. This paralysis eventually acquired a name: it became known as 'quiet diplomacy'.

Meanwhile, Mugabe went about systematically terrorising the supporters of the opposition – the agents of the African Renaissance – and wrecked his country's economy, with predictable results. A quarter of Zimbabwe's people fled to neighbouring countries, that is, Zambia, Malawi, Mozambique and Botswana, and especially to its bigger and richer neighbour, South Africa. The South African government estimates that approximately 2 million Zimbabweans now live in the country, mainly as illegal immigrants.[6]

Let us imagine that as a result of certain actions by a Chinese government 100 million Chinese people took flight to India, another 100 million poured into Russia and a further 100 million into Japan. The outcome of this influx would be predictable. India, Russia and Japan would form a military alliance and, in no time, their armies would force out the offending regime in Beijing. Proportionately, those 300 million Chinese equate to the size of the population that has fled Zimbabwe's economic and political crises and taken refuge in neighbouring countries.

Why the support for Mugabe?

Far from the governments of Zimbabwe's neighbouring states calling the Zanu-PF government to order, they take every available opportunity to wine, dine and laud President Robert Mugabe. They even go so far as to expect that the rest of the world follow their example. For example, southern African governments demanded that Mugabe be invited by Portugal to attend the Europe–Africa Summit held in Lisbon in December 2008, despite the travel ban imposed by the

European Union on Mugabe and his cronies. And in 2008 the South African government mobilised China and Russia to use their veto at the United Nations Security Council to protect the Zimbabwean government from censure for its human rights violations.

A question frequently asked by observers of the situation is why governments of other southern African states continue to turn a blind eye to the excesses of Robert Mugabe and his Zanu-PF?

The simple answer is short-sighted leadership coupled with the fear of the emergence of more democratic political forces in Zimbabwe that might threaten the status quo of southern Africa's established political elites. The case of Zimbabwe brings into sharp focus the fact that Africa's political elites can survive and even thrive under conditions of minimal domestic production.

As Zimbabwean society became increasingly sophisticated and its citizens better educated and more prosperous they demanded a greater say in how their country was run. The spectre of new, well-organised, cosmopolitan and vocal constituencies no longer interested in the politics of race but in the accountability of governance struck fear into the hearts of these elites and explains their solidarity with Zanu-PF and Mugabe.

Southern Africa is unique in Africa in that most of the

countries in the region are still ruled by the nationalist parties that fought against colonialism. These ruling parties – be they Zanu-PF in Zimbabwe, the Popular Movement for the Liberation of Angola (MPLA), the Chama Cha Mapinduzi (CCM) in Tanzania, the Liberation Front of Mozambique (Frelimo), the Botswana Democratic Party (BDP), the ANC in South Africa or the South West Africa People's Organisation (Swapo) in Namibia – consider that they are entitled to rule their countries forever by virtue of having been part of the liberation struggle. The attitude of these nationalist parties to the mass of the people is paternalistic and they do not accept that they should be accountable to them.

Such an attitude is, of course, myopic and largely futile. Nationalist parties and their governments in southern Africa can no more stop the march of progress and history than the colonialists before them could.

A new type of party

On 11 September 1999 the Zimbabwe Congress of Trade Unions (ZCTU), with the support of non-profit civil society organisations, established the Movement for Democratic Change (MDC), a new political party in Zimbabwe. The MDC's key objectives were to fight for a more democratic Constitution, to combat corruption and to reorganise the grossly mismanaged national economy, which was being manipulated to benefit Zimbabwe's political elite.

The new party received support from many prominent Zimbabweans in the professions, trade, industry, media and agriculture. The ZCTU allowed two of its leaders to join the new party – its general secretary, Morgan Tsvangirai, became president and Gibson Sibanda, ZCTU president, became the MDC's deputy president.

The rise of the MDC illustrated more than any other event to date the arrival of the African Renaissance. Nineteen years before, when Zimbabwe became independent, its social structure was simple and its social classes were largely defined by race. At the apex of the social pyramid were the whites, who controlled the economy, the professions and the mass media, in an alliance between the public and the private sector.

Below that apex was an intermediate stratum, barely differentiated, made up of wage earners, many of them migrant workers from the peasantry, with a sprinkle of semi-professionals and professionals, who acted as teachers, nurses, a few doctors and lawyers, shopkeepers, salespeople, and so on. At the bottom of the pyramid was a vast mass of undifferentiated peasants, who eked a living off the land.

By 2000 the country was transformed into a society with a rich and complex social structure. New black players were prominent in business, the mass media and other professions, as well as in organised labour and civil society in general. One of the largest cellular telephone operators in Africa, Econet, was founded by a black Zimbabwean.

In this rapidly changing and dynamic environment it was the ruling party, Zanu-PF, which remained unchanged. In fact, it fossilised.

Within one year of its establishment, in February 2000, the MDC, with the support of its civil-society allies, defeated Zanu-PF in a referendum over whether or not to adopt a new, more democratic Constitution. The new Constitution would have dramatically reduced the power of the president and would have abolished the 30 unelected members of parliament appointed by the president.

This caused panic among southern African rulers. A new type of party had emerged in the region, created by the people and therefore not controlled by the African elites.

From rebirth to near death

At independence, as detailed above, Zimbabwe had one of the most diversified economies in Africa. Today it is breaking every negative economic indicator imaginable. Life expectancy has fallen below 40 years; a quarter of the population has fled; inflation has reached numbers that boggle the mind; agricultural and manufacturing output are a fraction of what they were only eight years ago.

Figure 4.5, which shows Zimbabwe's per capita income trends in constant 1990 Zimbabwe dollars, indicates that the country has followed the economic trajectory after independence of most African countries. The first ten years showed a strong improvement in economic performance and per capita incomes. The next eight saw the economy marking time at lower levels. Thereafter there was a catastrophic economic collapse accompanied by political conflicts, capital and skills flight and the disintegration of food, manufacturing and mining production.

Zimbabweans are not the only people who are suffering as a result of Zanu-PF's follies. South Africans are also negatively affected, as are citizens of several other countries in the region.

Initially, as the economy stagnated it sucked in South African exports, but this benefit was to prove short lived. As the economy and social peace spiralled downwards South Africa's exports followed suit (see Figure 4.6). South Africa's exports to Zimbabwe in rands fell from R5 825 billion in 1997 to R4 854.3 billion in 2000.

Economic indicators are only one measure of a country's success or failure. A far more painful indicator of economic collapse is the health status and general well-being of the

Figure 4.5 **Zimbabwe's GDP per capita (1965–2008)**

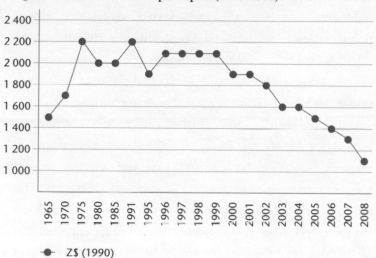

Source: Tony Hawkins, unpublished lectures, 2009.

Figure 4.6 **South African trade with Zimbabwe (1994–2001)**

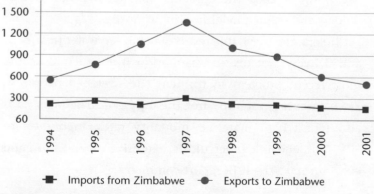

Source: Central Statistical Office, Harare, and the IMF.

population. If there were any doubts that once-prosperous Zimbabwe had become a failed state, a research report published early in 2009 by Physicians for Human Rights (PHR) would quell them. The report tells the sad story of nearly 30 years of economic, social and political meltdown under the rule of Zanu-PF, Zimbabwe's liberator.[7]

When the team of distinguished international physicians visited Zimbabwe in December 2008 on a fact-finding mission they found a country that was literally in the throes of an agonising death. The medical school and the two top hospitals in Harare, one of which was the teaching hospital, were closed – an almost unprecedented situation in the history of the modern world. Meanwhile, the country was in the grip of a cholera epidemic which had started in September 2008 and was spreading like wildfire. By the beginning of 2009 the epidemic had crossed Zimbabwe's borders and entered neighbouring countries.

Cholera, the inevitable result of collapsed water treatment and delivery systems and sanitation infrastructure, is the most recent problem to torment the wretched people of Zimbabwe. It is certainly not the only one. The physicians also found high maternal mortality rates, high rates of HIV/Aids, endemic tuberculosis, extensive malnutrition and even anthrax. The PHR report comments:

A causal chain runs from Mugabe's economic policies, to Zimbabwe's economic collapse, food insecurity and malnutrition, and the current outbreaks of infectious disease. These policies include the land seizures of 2000, a failed monetary policy and currency devaluations, and a cap on bank withdrawals. Mugabe's land seizures destroyed Zimbabwe's agricultural sector, which provided 45% of the country's foreign exchange revenue and livelihood for more than 70% of the population. Hyperinflation has ensued while salary levels have not kept pace. A government physician in Harare showed PHR her official pay stub; her monthly gross income in November 2008 was worth 32 US cents ($0.32 USD). The unemployment rate is over 80%. Low income households have had to reduce the quantity and quality of food. The Mugabe Zanu-PF government must be held accountable for the violation of the right to be free from hunger.[8]

It is therefore no accident that Zimbabwe today has the lowest life expectancy in the world. Life expectancy at birth has fallen from 62 years for both sexes in 1990 to 34 years in 2008.

Another important indicator of Zimbabwe's failure as a state is the way in which tuberculosis is being managed, or, more accurately, not managed:

PHR asked an expert working with the national program to

125

describe the status of the program in December 2008: 'There is no politically correct way to say this – the TB program in Zimbabwe is a joke. The national TB lab has one staff person. There is no one trained in drug sensitivity testing. The TB reference lab is just not functioning. This is a brain drain problem. The lab was working well until 2006 and has since fallen apart. The DOTS program in 2000 was highly effective, but that has broken down now too. There is no real data collection system for TB. This stopped in 2006 as well. Both MDR-TB and possible XDR-TB (a largely fatal and often untreatable form of the disease) have emerged in Zimbabwe, but there is no capacity either to diagnose or to manage these infections.[9]

Zimbabwe, once a beautiful and promising country, is now truly on its knees because of the greed of its political elite. A lack of investment has meant that its production capacity has seized up and funds that should have gone to building that capacity have been squandered on the private consumption of the elite and on its need to build up its repressive machinery.

While the political elite continues to live in luxury, while the First Lady indulges in obscene shopping trips abroad, the vast majority of Zimbabweans live in despair – starving, ill and increasingly without hope of ever having hope.

Change on the horizon?

From September 1999, after the emergence of the MDC as the leading opposition party in Zimbabwe, the incumbent Zanu-PF government went to great lengths to manipulate and rig successive elections.[10] These efforts were ultimately defeated in the March 2007 parliamentary election in which support for the MDC at the polls was so overwhelming that despite the efforts of Zanu-PF the MDC emerged as the winner.

The result of the presidential election, however, was less clear cut, with Morgan Tsvangirai failing to win the requisite number of votes to avoid a run-off. Unfortunately, during the period leading up to the run-off the violence unleashed against MDC supporters was so extensive that Tsvangirai declined to participate.

Mugabe, now the sole presidential candidate, declared himself president, a decision endorsed by the African Union. This created a stalemate, with the MDC controlling parliament but Zanu-PF controlling the presidency.

In February 2009, after lengthy negotiations mediated by South Africa's then president, Thabo Mbeki, and in terms of what was known as the Global Political Agreement (GPA), Mugabe, Tsvangirai and Arthur Mutambara, leader of a breakaway faction of the MDC, formed a coalition government in which Zanu-PF would have fifteen ministries, Tsvangirai's

MDC thirteen and Mutambara's faction three. Tsvangirai would be prime minister with Mutambara his deputy.

Could this be the breakthrough that would begin to haul Zimbabwe back from the disastrous path the Zanu-PF government had been following for the past decade? Many objective observers of the Zimbabwean situation are sceptical.

In an interview with the London-based *Financial Times* on 8 March 2009 Botswana's President Ian Khama was less than enthusiastic about the formation of the unity governments in Zimbabwe and Kenya. Khama pointed out that power-sharing agreements cobbled together between a former ruling party that has lost an election but insists on staying in power and an opposition party that has actually won the election is a recipe for disaster and a bad precedent for Africa.

Commenting specifically on the Zimbabwean situation, Khama said: 'If you had asked me to put together a combination of people who could spell disaster, that [pairing of Mugabe and Tsvangirai] would probably be the combination ... There is no love lost between them. I think they are really going to struggle.'[11]

Prior to signing the GPA Mugabe insisted that all parties to the negotiations accept that the seizure of commercial farms that had begun in February 2000 was irreversible. Effectively this means that the coalition government has no power to make policies about the core engine of the Zimbabwean economy – commercial agriculture.

This explains President Khama's scepticism about the new coalition government's ability to solve the country's problems. This is why Western powers are also unwilling to give financial support to the new regime.

It remains to be seen whether the sceptics will be proved wrong. In the meantime, seizures of commercial farms continue unabated and poverty and unemployment are still rife.

CHAPTER 5

THE FAILURE OF REGIONAL INTEGRATION

AFTER SEVERAL CENTURIES OF CAPITALISM FEW PEOPLE CANNOT CLAIM to know what must be done to develop a modern economy. The formula boils down to four simple requirements:

- ❏ Citizens must save.
- ❏ Entrepreneurs must invest these savings profitably.
- ❏ Entrepreneurs must take risks in the market place.
- ❏ The country must have a pool of workers with no choice but to sell their labour in order to live.

Whether or not these requirements are met in a particular

country at a particular time is, of course, quite another matter. An interesting illustration is the comparative situations of the United States of America and Haiti. The two countries became independent at about the same time by defeating their powerful colonisers in battle. Today they are at opposite ends of the development league tables. The United States is the most developed country in the world; Haiti is one of the poorest and least developed. The former country followed the requirements listed above; the latter did not.

A failure to follow the four requirements has been the case with most of the countries in sub-Saharan Africa. In previous chapters I have explored what has happened and continues to happen to Africa's savings, concluding that, far from being invested profitably, they are being consumed by political elites who use their positions of power to maintain extravagant lifestyles or to fund state machinery and, in many cases, repressive instruments of state.

Many of the savings are spirited away, usually illegally, by the political elites into offshore bank accounts and assets. Africa's entrepreneurs are, therefore, left with very little to invest and use to develop their countries' economies. Similarly, a large portion of the pool of potential workers remains locked into peasant farming in the small-scale agricultural sector or swarms into cities to live in informal settlements, either unemployed or self-employed in occupations that can barely sustain them and their families.

Thanks to their greed and ineptitude, Africa's political elites, unable to develop their countries' economies, have looked for panaceas or for a magic wand that they hoped would do the trick. Foreign aid was one such panacea, as was foreign investment in agriculture or mineral exports.

After African countries began to gain independence between the mid-1950s and the mid-1960s regional integration was touted as another miracle cure for the continent's underdevelopment. Accordingly, Africa is littered with organisations considered to be building blocks of an African common market or economic community: the Economic Community of West African States (Ecowas), the Southern African Development Community (SADC), the Common Market for Eastern and Southern Africa (Comesa), the African Union (AU), the New Partnership for Africa's Development (Nepad), the East African Community (EAC).

The alphabet soup of names promoting regional integration is long and dazzling. The results, however, are nowhere to be seen.

The theory behind the creation of these regional integration organisations is that European colonists fragmented Africa into many states, most of which were not economically viable. If there was to be capitalist economic development in these states, and therefore in Africa as a whole, several countries must be grouped together to create large markets without restrictions such as duties. Eventually such groupings should culminate in the creation of a continent-wide common market along the lines of the multi-member European Union, and one government along the lines of the United States.

All this is wishful thinking, as I argue below, because Africa does not have the material and political conditions that led to the emergence of the European Union.

The Organization of African Unity (OAU) was formed in 1963 with the specific mission of liberating those parts of Africa that remained under colonial rule and apartheid domination, though some would have wished it to be more ambitious and bring into being a united states of Africa. The OAU was replaced in 2002 by the African Union (AU), the change of name reflecting a change of direction – Africa's model for regional integration is now the European Union rather than the United States of America (although the AU's head as of 2 February 2009, Libya's Muammar Qaddafi, is set on the creation of a United States of Africa).

This should immediately tell us something about plans for regional integration in Africa – they are not home-grown, rather they are a copy of other people's efforts and, like many imitations, African regionalism is a superficial movement that is unlikely to achieve many of its architects' stated objectives.

Some lessons from Europe

The integration of Europe, a process that is not yet complete, resulted from the recognition by its countries' leaders that if their countries did not do something to modify the founding principles of the sovereign rights of states, the continent would, sooner or later, tear itself apart. In less than three generations, between 1870 and 1945, two of Europe's most powerful states, France and Germany, had fought three wars, each more devastating than the one before. The advent of nuclear weapons brought home the message that urgent steps had to be taken to avert another war between European powers. Regional integration was seen as inevitable.

Western Europe, especially after the Second World War, also faced the threat of being engulfed by Soviet communism and by home-grown communist insurrections in such important countries as France, Spain, Italy and Greece.

As it emerged from the war Europe did not have the power to defend itself, so it turned to the United States, both for military protection and for assistance in regenerating its shattered economy.

The Americans were glad to help as they felt that Soviet

expansionism, especially into the industrial heartlands of Europe, threatened their interests as well. Believing that the many countries of Europe, which were forever at one another's throats, could not be strong partners in its struggle against the Soviet Union, the United States demanded a strong element of regional integration from Europe as a condition for providing it with a nuclear umbrella.

The entrenched states of Europe, which had been in existence for centuries, had physical control over their territories and, above all, managed their political, social and economic systems. By the mid-twentieth century most of them had achieved similar levels of economic development and their populations enjoyed comparable standards of living. There were, of course, exceptions, such as the Iberian Peninsula and parts of southern Europe, which lagged behind, but these could be pulled up by the rest of Europe at minimum cost by means of a variety of targeted subsidies.

This industrial uniformity made it possible for Europe to implement trade liberalisation measures, the cornerstone of regional integration, with relatively little fear of some countries' economies and industries being swamped by those of their more developed partners.

The colonial state

By contrast with the countries of Europe, most of the African states we know in the first decade of the twenty-first century were artificial constructs created not by Africans but by foreign conquerors to facilitate their exploitation of the people of Africa and the continent's natural resources.

With a few exceptions, among them Egypt, Ethiopia, Liberia, Sierra Leone and, to some extent, South Africa, the different countries were created by European imperial powers in the wake of the Berlin Conference of 1884–85. Africans did not begin to gain control of their countries and their destiny until the 1960s.

African states, therefore, suffer a number of significant handicaps, among them the fact that many of their citizens do not feel they owe a strong allegiance to their country. This partly explains why, since the 1960s, they have been the sites of many conflicts, particularly civil wars, inter-tribal wars, violent communal conflicts and pogroms, wars of secession and, more recently, in the Great Lakes region of central Africa and in parts of the Sudan, genocide and ethnic cleansing. These conflicts have been accompanied by vast population movements across several national boundaries. Africa is host to the largest number of refugees and internally displaced persons in the world.[1]

The comparatively recent accession of African rulers has led to a perception among African elites that sovereignty is a valuable economic asset which enables them to enrich themselves. It is this attitude that exacerbates the lack of allegiance of many to their country given that the process of elite self-enrichment undermines the state's ability to deliver effective social services.

An important characteristic of conflicts in Africa, and one that distinguishes them from those in Europe, has been the almost complete absence of inter-state wars – the fear of which was one of the driving forces behind European regional integration. In the past 50 years there have been only two inter-state wars among African countries – that between Tanzania and Uganda in the 1970s and between Ethiopia and Eritrea in the 1990s. The latter could, in fact, be considered to have been a continuation of the secessionist war of Eritrean rebels from Ethiopia.

Inter-state wars have, however, been an important factor in nation building, especially in Europe. Conflicts between states, which pose a threat to all citizens, irrespective of race, tribe, class, religious affiliation and so on, give rise to a number of unintended consequences.

Firstly, they strengthen the hold of the ruling class, and of the state it controls, over the general population, which, faced with an external threat, is compelled to surrender more and more of its autonomy to the state and its agents as a way of strengthening national defence and limiting dissension. This gives the rule of the rulers legitimacy, as they are seen as defenders of all the people.

Secondly, the state is forced to become better organised in order to raise and equip its armed forces while at the same time maintaining or even increasing production to sustain both the war effort and the civilian population.

Thirdly, inter-state wars compel the dominant ruling faction(s) to make concessions to more marginalised factions in order to build a united front with which to confront the foreign enemy. Inter-state wars thus contribute to reducing or moderating various forms of discrimination against minorities.

By contrast, the intra-state conflicts that characterise Africa have resulted in the fragmentation of societies into warring factions and parties, and have made even more tenuous the already fragile allegiance of large sections of the population to the state and to those who control the state. Far from the state emerging strengthened from intra-state conflicts, it is weakened by them. A large number of its technocrats are killed or exiled and many institutions are ruined – permeated with corruption and manned by unqualified and underqualified personnel.

This brings us to an important fact about why states

have proved to be largely ineffectual in promoting Africa's development process. States in Europe and Asia evolved over centuries and a great deal of experimentation went into establishing them. The result was a Europe consisting of uni-ethnic states managed by a professional class of officials governed by complex rules and regulations designed to combat favouritism and other disintegrating forces. These laws enabled the state machinery to appear open and accessible and therefore to be operating fairly and in the interests of all members of society, with no segment of that society excluded from holding a position in the state machinery.

All these features helped to legitimate the European state in the eyes of most of its citizens and therefore to make it worth fighting for.

The new scramble for Africa

The 1950s and 1960s saw a move by a small African political elite to capture the colonial state. One of the great pioneers of this scramble for power on the eve of Africa's independence, Ghana's Dr Kwame Nkrumah, urged the emerging political elites: 'Seek ye first the political kingdom and all else shall be added onto you.'[2]

The result is that the history of Africa since the 1960s is

the history of groups of elites seeking the 'political kingdom' with the primary purpose of enriching themselves. Built into this quest for wealth has been the exclusion of outsiders – the mass of the population and weak sections of the political elite whose inclusion would reduce the benefits accruing to the dominant group or groups of elites. Genocide, ethnic cleansing, tribalism, regionalism, religious extremism and so on were the logical outcomes of the intra-elite competition to control the colonial state.

These intra-elite conflicts also undermined the emergence of a ruling class with a unitary vision and consensus over the means of creating a prosperous country. Most countries of sub-Saharan Africa, therefore, do not, even today, have ruling classes. Africa is ruled by an ever-changing mosaic of political elites, who maintain themselves in power by excluding other elites. They sustain and reproduce themselves by perpetuating the neo-colonial state and its attendant socio-economic systems of exploitation, devised by European colonialists.

Constraints on regional trade integration

Since the 1960s vast amounts of time and money have been expended on promoting regional integration in Africa, with little to show for it. The pathetically low trade flows among African countries have largely remained unchanged from what they were a generation ago, despite all the energy that has been devoted to regional cooperation and integration. This is evident from Table 5.1, which shows that the Southern African Customs Union (SACU) – which comprises South Africa, Botswana, Lesotho, Swaziland and Namibia – is the only significant economic player; within the SACU, South Africa is unquestionably the dominant country.

We have seen that European countries, big and small, had achieved a high level of industrialisation and economic development long before regional trade integration was high on their agenda. It was political and security issues rather than economic development issues that drove European integration, just as it was in Asia, where one of the oldest regional organisations, the Association of South East Asian Nations, was inspired more by the common fear of communism than by economic development objectives.

By contrast, in Africa the need for regional integration is based on economic rather than political or security issues.

As we have seen above, Africa's political elites argue that most African countries are small, poor and underdeveloped, and therefore lack domestic markets. To compensate for these shortcomings, the argument goes, it is necessary for them to eliminate barriers to trade among themselves. By doing so, it is said, they will be able to develop enterprises with the

Table 5.1 **Total intra-SADC trade (exports and imports)**

SADC countries	As a share of intra-SADC exports, 1992 (%)	As a share of intra-SADC exports, 2002 (%)
Angola	0.55	0.23
Democratic Republic of Congo (DRC)	2.64	0.99
Malawi	2.50	1.66
Mauritius	0.63	0.65
Mozambique	1.40	3.33
Seychelles	0.04	0.12
SACU	70.90	77.32
Tanzania	0.72	1.08
Zambia	3.19	4.88
Zimbabwe	17.43	9.74

SADC countries	As a share of intra-SADC imports, 1992 (%)	As a share of intra-SADC imports, 2002 (%)
Angola	5.28	7.43
Democratic Republic of Congo (DRC)	5.83	4.17
Malawi	9.01	9.56
Mauritius	7.15	7.29
Mozambique	11.86	10.50
Seychelles	1.12	1.15
SACU	18.54	12.74
Tanzania	3.36	5.24
Zambia	9.60	16.15
Zimbabwe	28.25	25.78

Source: African Development Bank Group. 2004. 'Regional Assistance Strategy Paper (2004–2008)', p. 9.[3]

requisite economies of scale to make them competitive in the world markets.

The experience of Europe, however, shows that this argument is flawed. Relatively small European countries – such as Sweden, Switzerland, the Netherlands, Denmark and Belgium – developed world-class companies long before European integration became a reality. Multinational corporations that developed in these small countries include Electrolux, Volvo, Saab, Nestlé, Philips, Unilever, Royal Dutch/Shell, Carling, Interbrew, Heineken, ABB, Ericsson, Nokia, Norsk Hydro, Roche, Maersk, UBS, ABN-AMRO, to name but a few.

Such examples show that it is not the size of a country's population that determines whether or not the country industrialises, rather it is its skills pool and its control over its economic and social policies that, in the final analysis, determine the level of industrialisation.

The key to development

The single most important factor determining the level of development of any country is the degree to which it is able to control its own political, economic and social space, and therefore its policies. In most African countries social, economic and, to a large extent, political policies are not controlled by Africans or, more accurately, by Africa's rulers;

they are controlled by foreigners who do so to the benefit of other foreigners. Among the most important non-African players determining African policies are:

❏ foreign multinational corporations, of which the most striking examples today are the oil companies, which run massive extractive industries in Africa with almost no links to the local economies in which they operate, apart from a trickle of royalties that pay for imports to finance elite consumption and to fuel corruption and repression;
❏ multilateral financial institutions which, by imposing various forms of conditions, dictate the economic and social policies of African states; and
❏ other foreign state and non-state players who, through their role as donors and/or creditors, have extensive leverage and therefore influence over the social and economic policies of African states.

Another important factor determining whether or not a country develops is its ability to generate a meaningful economic surplus and to direct a large part of that surplus to productive investment rather than to private consumption. A large part of sub-Saharan Africa's surplus leaves the continent as debt repayment, expatriation of profit, capital flight, and so on.

One of the most disgraceful but underreported scandals in Africa is the extent to which African elites export capital from the continent. According to the Commission for Africa, nearly 40 per cent of Africa's private wealth is kept outside Africa, compared to only 3 per cent of South Asia's private wealth and 6 per cent of East Asia's.[4] The small economic surplus that remains, as we have seen, goes to finance elite consumption and to pay for the running of the largely unaccountable state.

These are some of the factors that explain the inability of sub-Saharan African states to train and retain the skilled people they need in order to embark on a sustainable industrialisation drive comparable to those of, for example, South and East Asia.

If we examine what happened in Western Europe in the past and what is happening in Asia now it appears that two engines drive development and industrialisation. These are policies that promote capital accumulation and investment in social capital – healthcare, education, public housing and social peace – and, in turn, lead to another outcome, the second main driver of Western European industrialisation and development in the past and of Asian industrialisation today – that is, competitiveness in world markets.

Similarly, it was the ability of small countries in Europe to compete in world markets that made it possible, long before

European integration made an appearance after the Second World War, to achieve the same levels of development as those of large countries, which had the advantage of bigger domestic markets.

A similar explanation would apply to Africa. It is the developmental domestic policies and practices of individual countries that will drive the continent's development in the first instance, not how neighbours cooperate. What happens between neighbours is important mainly for reasons of political stability, but what will drive African economic development is the quality of relations between individual African countries and the world market. (African markets are of course subsumed in world markets.) In the African context Mauritius is a good illustration of a small country that has followed the developmental model of Western European countries of a similar size, exploiting world markets to develop its own industries.

At independence in the 1960s Mauritius was typical of many African countries with a small land mass and a small population. It had a single-crop economy (sugar), which accounted for most of its export earnings and formal employment, a multi-ethnic society and low per capita incomes. Today it is, next to South Africa, Africa's economic giant, the richest non-oil-producing country on the continent, boasting an economy that is almost as diversified as that of

South Africa and per capita incomes that now surpass those in South Africa.[5]

This phenomenal progress was not achieved through regional integration; it was driven largely by competitively priced high-quality clothing and textile exports to world markets and by building a world-class tourist industry that catered for high-paying Western customers.

* * *

Today Mauritius and South Africa are important investors in other African countries. They have achieved this position primarily because they have been able to grow and diversify their economies by taking advantage of their domestic markets and, above all, by being major players in world markets.

The strength of these two countries is also contributing to driving the integration of the economies of southern Africa. As Table 5.1 above shows, Mauritius, despite its small population, is a bigger player in intra-SADC imports than other SADC countries such as Angola, the DRC and Tanzania, which have populations that are many times larger. The same applies to South Africa, which accounts for more than 70 per cent of intra-SADC exports.

In addition to their role as relatively large trading partners with their neighbours, Mauritius and South Africa provide a technology and skills transfer that contributes to the economies of the region as a whole – many businesses within southern Africa, for example, tourism, sugar, retail, telecommunications, manufacturing, banking and mining, owe their existence to these two countries.

South Africa plays another invisible but critical role in promoting regional integration. Each year more than 40 000 students from other African countries, especially from SADC countries, study at South African universities.[6] South Africa also provides other forms of training enabling citizens of SADC countries to acquire skills they are later able to use in their home countries.

CHAPTER 6

AFRICA NEEDS A NEW DEMOCRACY

IN HIS ACCLAIMED 2007 WORK *The Bottom Billion: Why the Poorest Countries are Failing and What Can Be Done About It*, Paul Collier concludes that while most of humanity has found ways to work its way out of poverty, there are a billion people in the world who are trapped in extreme penury. The majority of these people are Africans, especially, according to Collier, the Africans who live south of the Sahara.

Collier identifies many factors that lock the mass of the people of sub-Saharan Africa into an apparently unbreakable cycle of grinding poverty. He also suggests several admirable solutions that the rest of the world community might put in place to bail out Africa.

This book is far less ambitious than Collier's. In it I have examined only one factor that contributes to keeping Africans in the bottom billion – the role played by Africa's rulers, the continent's political elites, in keeping their fellow citizens poor, as well as how these elites benefit from Africa's poverty traps and what needs to be done to break their stranglehold on political power and set sub-Saharan Africa on the road to development.

Collier touches on this issue in his discussion of the role of governments in keeping the people of sub-Saharan Africa in the bottom billion. He writes:

> The prevailing conditions bring out extremes. Leaders are sometimes psychopaths who have shot their way to power, sometimes crooks who have bought it, and sometimes brave people who, against the odds, are trying to build a better future. Even the appearance of modern governments in these states is sometimes a façade, as if the leaders are reading from a script. They sit at the international negotiating tables, such as the World Trade Organization, but they have nothing to negotiate. The seats stay occupied even in the face of melt-down in their societies: the government of Somalia continued to be officially 'represented' in the international arena for years after Somalia ceased to have a functioning government in the country itself. So don't expect the governments of the

> bottom billion to unite in forming a practical agenda: they
> are fractured between villains and heroes, and some of them
> are barely there. For our future world to be livable the heroes
> must win their struggle. But the villains have the guns and
> the money and, to date they have usually prevailed. That will
> continue unless we radically change our approach.[1]

Africa's multitudinous problems have become a matter of concern to many people throughout the world. The prestigious American think tank, the Brookings Institution, released a report in 2008 entitled *Index of State Weakness in the Developing World*. The authors, Susan E. Rice and Stewart Patrick, found that of the 28 'critically weak' states in the developing world, 23 are in sub-Saharan Africa.

They define weak states as countries that 'lack the essential capacity and/or will to fulfil four sets of critical government responsibilities: fostering an environment conducive to sustainable and equitable economic growth; establishing and maintaining legitimate transparent, and accountable political institutions; securing their populations from violent conflict and controlling their territory; and meeting the basic human needs of their population'.[2]

With this checklist as a guide I conclude that only a handful of countries in Africa pass muster on most counts. The top twenty performers among the 141 countries surveyed include only two in Africa – Seychelles[3] and Mauritius. South Africa's high crime and HIV/Aids infection rate relegate it to 110th place. Bottom of the list is Somalia, the world's number one failed state.

Pseudo-states

Why it is that after half a century of managing their countries' affairs Africa's political elites have proved so incapable of addressing their political and developmental challenges? Put another way, what was it that the political elites inherited at independence that makes them underperform so glaringly in the development race?

Most analysts of post-colonial Africa assume that at independence African nationalists inherited a state. The assumption is erroneous – what they inherited was a government. If the Marxists are correct that under the capitalist system the state can be described as the executive committee of the bourgeoisie, the states created by the colonial powers were, in reality, merely pseudo-states, since, strictly speaking, the African colonies had no bourgeoisie as such.

In 'The Manifesto of the Communist Party' Karl Marx and Friedrich Engels wrote: 'The executive of the modern State is but a committee for managing the common affairs of the whole bourgeoisie.'[4] African nationalists themselves were

154

neither a capitalist class nor a bourgeoisie so their 'executive committee', while it might resemble a state, is not one. As controllers of the pseudo-state, that is, the post-colonial governments, Africa's political elites do not control their countries or their economies. As a purely government class they are consumers, not producers, as are the true bourgeoisie, and therefore they cannot make economic development happen. In most of Africa, I contend, the economy remains in the hands of the peasants and of foreign investors, a thesis that is discussed in the preceding chapters.

As explained in Chapter 1, the fact that peasants and foreign investors lack the political power to protect their savings from being confiscated and consumed by the political elites is a fundamental reason for Africa's economic underdevelopment. Conversely, it is only the two African countries with a home-grown bourgeoisie – Mauritius and South Africa – that have made significant economic headway, although, as we have seen in the case of South Africa, this is now threatened.

According to Marx and Engels the bourgeoisie are the only group that can create a thriving capitalist system or a developed modern state. As they put it:

> Historically it [the bourgeoisie] has played a most revolutionary part. The bourgeoisie, wherever it has got the upper hand,

155

has put an end to all feudal, patriarchal, idyllic relations ...

It has accomplished wonders far surpassing Egyptian pyramids, Roman aqueducts, and Gothic cathedrals ...

The bourgeoisie has through its exploitation of the world market given a cosmopolitan character to production and consumption in every country ... All old-established national industries have been destroyed or are daily being destroyed. They are dislodged by new industries, whose introduction becomes a life and death question for all civilised nations ... In place of the old wants, satisfied by the production of the country, we find new wants, requiring for their satisfaction the products of distant lands and climes ...

National one-sidedness and narrow-mindedness become more and more impossible, and from the numerous national and local literatures there arises a world literature. The bourgeoisie, by the rapid improvement of all instruments of production, by the immensely facilitated means of communication, draws all, even the most barbarian, nations into civilisation.[5]

The non-development of sub-Saharan African countries is clearly attributable to the fact that under colonialism they did not develop an indigenous bourgeoisie. The character of the elites that inherited political power from the colonists and continue to hold it half a century after independence militates against the emergence of a bourgeoisie in Africa. This issue was discussed in Chapter 1.

The case of South Africa is different in that it does have a bourgeoisie – one that began to emerge at the start of the twentieth century and whose growth was accelerated during the long reign of the National Party. One of the unintended consequences of economic sanctions against South Africa was that the ownership of the mines and the banks, originally in the hands of the British, eventually ended up in the hands of an indigenous bourgeoisie (referred to in previous chapters as the economic oligarchy).

With the advent of parliamentary democracy in 1994, South Africa's real bourgeoisie, through the process of Black Economic Empowerment (which is discussed in Chapter 3), created a new class from among the African National Congress (ANC) politicians. But it is a pseudo-bourgeoisie whose purpose is to act primarily as an interlocutor in the inner circles of the new political elite on behalf of the real bourgeoisie. Like the pseudo-states in sub-Saharan Africa, these pseudo-bourgeoisie are not a class of entrepreneurs. At best they are crony capitalists who are patronised by the economic oligarchy, just as Africa's pseudo-states are patronised by Western powers through foreign aid.

An article in Johannesburg's *Business Day* in January 2009 by Michael Spicer, executive director of Business Leadership

South Africa, the organisation that represents the largest corporations in South Africa, would seem to back up this thesis. Writing about the unseating of the country's former president, Thabo Mbeki, Spicer names two former ANC politicians, now among South Africa's richest men, Tokyo Sexwale and Cyril Ramaphosa, as active participants in the decision:

> It was Cyril Ramaphosa, backed by Tokyo Sexwale who led the charge at the meeting of the ANC's national executive committee, which decided to defenestrate Mbeki in September last year. These two capitalists remain embedded in the ANC leadership, joining another politician turned businessman Mathews Phosa who has long been a staunch Zuma supporter. These three ... and many others remain within the ANC structure to counter the desire of the SACP/ Cosatu for a strong leftwards shift in policy.[6]

New partnerships for Africa's development

In the four to five decades of their independence African countries have gone through a wrenching period, as a result of which a number of negative factors have become dominant:

❏ Countries lost key indigenous institutions that had been created by Africans themselves to fight against colonialism. These were the nationalist parties, independent trade unions, civil society organisations and independent institutions of learning, all of them crushed by the military dictators who took control of African governments in the 1960s in collaboration with Western powers. Even in countries where the military did not take over, nationalist parties degenerated into one-man rule.

❏ With the exception of the economies in South Africa and Mauritius, African economies failed to break away from the economic model created by colonialism; consequently, African producers did not regain their autonomy but continued to be dominated by the political elite that controlled the state. The new political class thus used its dominance over the producers to siphon savings from them to the political elite and the state, especially its repressive instruments. According to one source, security forces in African countries collectively number more than 2 million and cost the continent an estimated US$14 billion annually.[7]

❏ The combination of either military or civilian dictatorships and the subordination of producers to the political elites led to the underdevelopment of a middle class as well as to a massive brain drain.

159

Can the New Partnership for Africa's Development (Nepad) change this lethal legacy? While Nepad may address some of the worst excesses of the political elites through its African Peer Review Mechanism, it does not tackle the fundamental malaise, that is, the enormous power imbalance between political elites and key private-sector producers.

If the driving force behind sub-Saharan Africa's under-development is the structural powerlessness of producers, and therefore their inability to retain and control their savings, it should be self-evident that until this equation is reversed there will be no development in sub-Saharan Africa.

If the African sub-continent is to develop, it needs a new type of democracy – a democracy that will empower not only the political elites but also the region's private-sector producers, most of whom are peasants. The new democracy should be able to restore the growth of an independent and productive middle class as well as facilitate the development of autonomous civil society institutions.

This change is starting to happen on a significant scale in southern Africa where, since the 1990s, a new and distinctive political and economic voice has emerged from trade unions, sections of business, civil society organisations and academics. This voice, which emerged in Zambia from 1990 with the creation of the Movement for Multi-Party Democracy (MMD) by the Zambian Congress of Trade Unions, addresses issues of inequality and poverty, and articulates the need for new economic and social thinking, as well as for governmental accountability. In Zambia the new movement succeeded, through the ballot box, in getting rid of the one-party regime of the United National Independence Party, which had ruled the country since independence in 1964.

The establishment of the MMD was followed in 1999 by the creation in Zimbabwe of another opposition party, the Movement for Democratic Change (MDC), also by a trade union movement – the Zimbabwe Congress of Trade Unions. As indicated in Chapter 4, the MDC has had a tougher time than the MMD, with many of its supporters killed, tortured, raped and maimed by members of the ruling Zimbabwe African National Union – Patriotic Front (Zanu-PF). The Zimbabwean story is still unfolding, with the most recent development being the establishment of a government incorporating both Zanu-PF and the opposition MDC, but the foundation has been laid in the relatively more industrialised countries of southern Africa, including South Africa, for the emergence of a new democracy.

Taking into consideration the broader sub-Saharan region, which is less industrialised, in the first instance it is necessary for peasants, who constitute the core of the private sector, to become the real owners of their primary asset – land. Until this happens there will be no change in the trend towards

161

rampant deforestation and accelerating desertification. In order to reverse this process, freehold land tenure must be introduced and the so-called communal land-tenure system, which is, in reality, state land ownership, must be abolished.

Secondly, peasant producers must gain direct access to world markets without the political elite, through state corporations, acting as the go-between. This means that internationally traded cash crops – coffee, tea, cotton, sugar, cocoa, rubber, and so on – must be auctioned by the producers themselves rather than being sold first to state-controlled marketing boards.

Another important and necessary innovation is new financial institutions independent of the political elite that will address the financial needs not only of peasants but also of other small- to medium-scale producers. These institutions could be co-operatives, credit unions or savings banks. Besides providing financial services they would undertake technical services, which are currently not being provided by the political elite, such as crop research, extension services, livestock improvement, storage, transportation and distribution, all of which would contribute to making agriculture in sub-Saharan Africa more productive.

It is in this area that foreign donors could play a constructive role – supporting these independent institutions by providing the expertise to manage them and, to some extent, helping to shield them from predators.

Such changes would, for the first time, bring into being in Africa a capitalist market economy that is responsive to the real needs of African producers and consumers. Before independence capitalism in Africa promoted the interests of colonialists; since independence it has promoted those of the parasitic political elites that control the state and believe that their survival is threatened by the emergence of an independent middle and professional class.

If Nepad is to contribute to Africa's economic development it should help to redesign the continent's political economy so that it promotes the interests of producers instead of those of the rent-seeking elites.

Sub-Saharan Africa could draw an important lesson from the agricultural reforms that have taken place in China in the past 25 years or so, which have made it possible for that country to embark on its current breakneck industrialisation process.[8] The breakthrough came with the recognition by the Chinese communists that the state alone could not industrialise the country. The government therefore opened the space for the emergence of an independent private sector driven by the middle and professional classes.

The situation in South Africa

What does the future hold for South Africa, the largest economy in Africa, if, as noted in Chapters 2 and 3, the country persists on the road mapped out in the past fifteen years by the black political elite and their allies among the mining- and finance-based economic oligarchy that has marginalised entrepreneurship and manufacturing in favour of consumption?

Economically South Africa is to Africa what the United States of America is to the rest of the world. Although it comprises only about 5 per cent of the African population of the continent, South Africa produces a quarter of Africa's Gross Domestic Product (GDP). This is where the comparison with the United States stops, however. While the United States continues to hold its own in the world league tables, South Africa is on a downward trajectory. The short-lived upward trend in the 2000s is already being impacted on by the current global economic crisis.

The figures below illustrate more than any number of words the difficulties that South Africa faces. Figure 6.1 compares South Africa's formal sector employment trend with that of developed countries as well as with equivalent middle-income countries, showing clearly that in South Africa the trend is going in the wrong direction – a situation resulting from South Africa's growing de-industrialisation

Figure 6.1 **Employment trends in South Africa and elsewhere (1980–2006)**

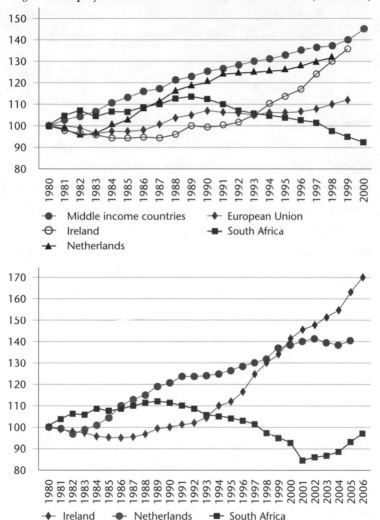

Source and ©: (Top): World Bank, World Development Indicators, from the WEFA dataset.[9]
(Bottom): ILO (International Labour Organization), International Labour Statistics. Nicoli
   Nattrass, 2008, unpublished.

in the face of fierce competition from Asian countries.

The country's de-industrialisation is reflected in the composition of its merchandise exports, as Figure 6.2 illustrates.

In 1990 raw materials – minerals, basic metals, basic chemicals and refinery products, as well as pulp and paper – comprised less than 40 per cent of South Africa's exports. By 2005 they constituted more than 60 per cent. Even the growing export of motor vehicles and parts is deceptive because the local content of South African-made vehicles is as low as 30 per cent, while most of the automotive parts the country exports are catalytic converters, whose primary value is the platinum they contain, thus making them another example of the power of the Minerals-Energy Complex (MEC) – South Africa has one of the world's largest platinum mining sectors. As the 'Other goods exports' category includes agricultural exports, the value of South Africa's manufactured exports is, in fact, lower than that shown in Figure 6.2.

South Africa's trade with its newest large trading partner, the People's Republic of China, reflects this growing de-industrialisation.

Figure 6.3 (on page 169) shows that nearly three-quarters of China's exports to South Africa are made up of manufactured products. The large machinery and car components category accounts for the decline in the local content of South African-

Figure 6.2 **Breakdown of South Africa's merchandise exports (1990–2005)**

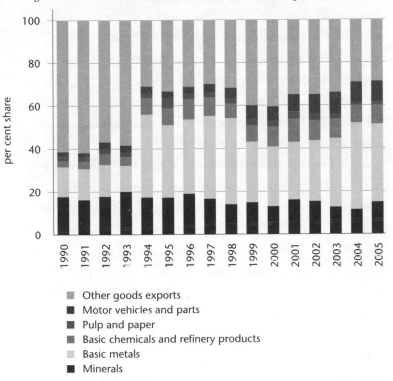

■ Other goods exports
■ Motor vehicles and parts
■ Pulp and paper
■ Basic chemicals and refinery products
■ Basic metals
■ Minerals

Source: Quantec Research, 2005.

made vehicles referred to above. South Africa's exports to China (see Figure 6.4 on page 170), by contrast, show very clearly that the relationship between the two countries consists of South Africa as a raw materials supplier to China, and China as a manufactured products supplier to South Africa. Not surprisingly, there is a large trade imbalance between the two countries in favour of China.

The de-industrialisation of South Africa has created a massive urban and rural underclass that can only be placated by welfare expenditure. This is not a new road; it has been travelled by other countries, among them Argentina and Algeria, with disastrous consequences.

Algeria became a land of promise because of rising oil prices in the 1970s, rather as South Africa is today, mesmerised as it is by rising mineral prices thanks to Asian industrialisation.

Algeria's paternalistic post-liberation elite channelled these high oil revenues in all directions, not least into its own consumption, but without creating entrepreneurs. The result was that unemployment, especially that of young people and graduates, grew in the 1980s, despite massive social expenditure by the government.

In 1991 the disaffected population, mobilised by the Islamic Salvation Front (FIS), was about to vote out the National Liberation Front (FLN), around which the elite in that country coalesced. In a panic, the army annulled the elections, with predictable results. In the ensuing civil war more than 200 000 people were killed – the brutality of the protagonists was as breathtaking as any in the Rwanda genocide.[10]

Of course, no two countries are alike, but South Africa

Figure 6.3 **China's exports to South Africa (2004)**

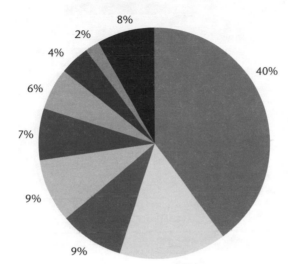

■ Machinery and car components (40%)
▢ Textiles (15%)
■ Footwear (9%)
▢ Chemical products (9%)
■ Agricultural produce (7%)
▢ Base metals or articles thereof (6%)
■ Mineral products (4%)
▢ Building material (2%)
■ Other manufactured products (8%)

Source: Emerging Market Focus (Pty) Ltd. 2004.

Figure 6.4 **South Africa's exports to China (2004)**

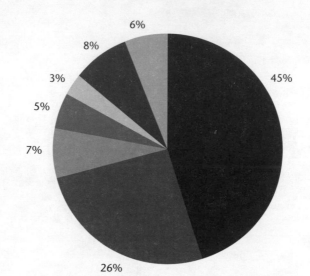

- Base metals and articles thereof – steel (45%)
- Mineral products (26%)
- Chemical products (7%)
- Paper pulp (5%)
- Basic raw materials (3%)
- Machinery, equipment, car and motor components (8%)
- Other (6%)

Source: Emerging Market Focus (Pty) Ltd. 2004.

170

has many of the ingredients that led to the explosion in Algeria: a complacent political elite that lives off liberation struggle history and mythology; vast natural resources, gold, platinum, coal, ferro-alloys, and so on, in place of Algeria's oil and gas; large revenues from these natural resources with which to feed the underclass and allow the elites to pocket the rest through various means, including corruption; and growing unemployment among young graduates in an economy that is not creating jobs.

All this is not to imply that what happened in Algeria will occur in South Africa. However, the Algerian situation might be regarded as an early warning signal. What can be done to avoid a similar scenario unfolding in South Africa?

Wanted: A mindset change

In the preceding chapters I have proffered an insight into the nature of sub-Saharan Africa's political elites – their origins, modus operandi and relationships with their fellow citizens, with the countries in their region, with the world beyond the African continent, and especially with their countries' main trading partners.

In doing so, I have identified two types of societies in sub-Saharan Africa – capitalist states and neo-colonial pseudo-states. Mauritius and South Africa are the closest examples

Africa has to functioning capitalist states or societies. The other countries in the sub-continent cannot be classified as capitalist states for an assortment of reasons, some given below, and therefore qualify only as neo-colonial pseudo-states.

Several features, past and present, distinguish capitalist states in Africa from non-capitalist ones:

❏ Capitalist states do not have a peasantry in their social structure, while the populations of neo-colonial countries are predominantly peasant-based.

❏ In the past those states that are now classified as capitalist imported slaves, while neo-colonial states exported slaves or indentured migrant labourers.

❏ Land in capitalist states is owned predominantly by private property owners, while in neo-colonial countries most of the land, especially agricultural land, is in the hands of the government.

❏ In capitalist states most of the means of production and exchange are owned largely by home-grown private capitalists or bourgeoisie; in neo-colonial states the main means of production and exchange are owned largely by foreigners and/or by the government.

Most African countries – again Mauritius and South Africa are exceptions – do not have a bourgeoisie, or, to put it another way, an entrepreneurial class, and it is this that lies at the heart of the continent's underdevelopment.

The two types of societies are, perforce, ruled differently, by groups with varied purposes aiming to achieve different outcomes.

The motivation of rulers of Africa's capitalist countries is to drive the process of capital accumulation, as is the case in most other capitalist countries, by maintaining the profitability of private enterprises. This requires several pre-conditions:

❑ Protection of private property rights.
❑ Rule of law.
❑ Diversity and growth of skills in the labour force.
❑ Cooperation between labour and management.
❑ A healthy labour force.
❑ A stable social and political environment.

The motivation of political elites in neo-colonial countries is very different. Their primary interest is not to promote capital accumulation – their countries do not have capitalists to do so – but to extract rents from the foreigners who, as noted above, control most of the means of production and exchange. These foreigners may be mining companies, oil companies or miscellaneous investors and traders. Another objective of political elites in neo-colonial countries is to extract whatever surplus they can from peasant agriculture.

What this tells us is that these elites are a rentier class – one whose income is derived from investments – and are thus parasitic on the limited productive capacity in their countries. This parasitism exacerbates the productive capacity problems of these countries, further contributing to their underdevelopment.

These elites have no sense of ownership of their country and are not interested in its development. They view the country primarily as a cash cow that enables them to live extravagantly on imported goods and services as they attempt to mimic the lifestyles of the colonialists. It is this mindset of non-ownership that largely accounts for sub-Saharan Africa's non-development and, as a consequence, its poverty. With the lack of a sense of ownership goes the pillaging of resources, neglect of the welfare of the people, corruption, capital flight and, ultimately, brutality against dissenting voices.

What then must be done, and by whom, either to change the mindset of existing political elites in neo-colonial countries or to replace them with leaders who are more oriented toward development? This is a question that is simple enough to pose but complex to answer.

In 1964, after a tour of several African countries, Chinese Prime Minister Zhou Enlai said: 'An excellent revolutionary situation exists in Africa.'[11] Premier Zhou did not say what type of revolution, but in the light of what has happened in China since his pronouncement, it would seem that what Africa needs first and foremost is a bourgeois revolution similar to that in China.

The first step towards achieving this is to throw open land ownership to the peasants on a freehold basis, a policy that would encourage them to invest in land improvement, thereby making it possible for them to accumulate funds to invest in other sectors of the economy. This is one revolution that can be achieved by the combined efforts of Africans, the East and the West.

'GUKURAHUNDI'

ON 12 AUGUST 1980 ROBERT MUGABE, THEN PRIME MINISTER OF Zimbabwe, announced in his Heroes' Day speech that former guerrillas would form a militia to be trained to combat 'malcontents', who were 'unleashing a reign of terror'.[1] In October Mugabe and North Korean President Kim Il Sung signed an agreement by which North Korea would train and arm this brigade.

In August 1981, 106 Korean instructors arrived to train the brigade, which was to be known as 5 Brigade, its purpose being solely to 'deal with dissidents and any other trouble in the country'. The crack squad would also be known as 'Gukurahundi', a Shona expression meaning 'the rain which washes away the chaff'.

From the start, the members of the 5 Brigade, most of them Shona-speaking Zimbabwe National Liberation Army (Zanla) forces loyal to the prime minister, made it clear that they were answerable to 'nobody but Mugabe' and regarded themselves as above the law.

Five Brigade was destined to become the most controversial army unit ever formed in Zimbabwe. Within weeks of being mobilised at the end of January 1983 it was responsible for the deaths of more than 2 000 civilians, the burning of hundreds of homesteads and thousands of beatings in the communal living areas of Northern Matabeleland, where hundreds of thousands of Zimbabwe African People's Union (Zapu) supporters lived.

Most of the dead were killed in public executions, involving between 1 and 12 people at a time. The largest number of dead in a single incident was recorded in Lupane, where 62 men and women were shot on the banks of the Cewale River on 5 March 1983. In another incident in Lupane, on 6 February, 52 villagers were shot in the small village of Silwane, mostly in small groups in the vicinity of their own homes. There were several incidents in Tsholotsho involving large numbers of casualties in each, many of them members of families burnt to death in huts.

The government had introduced a stringent set of curfew regulations in Tsholotsho, Nyama-ndlovu, Lupane, Nkayi,

Bubi and Dete, all in Matabeleland North, to coincide with the arrival of 5 Brigade. These regulations severely limited movement into and around the curfew areas. In addition, stores were closed and deliveries of food for drought relief suspended. All forms of transport were banned, including bicycles and scotch carts. Those found breaking the curfew regulations risked being shot.

A near-total information blackout ensured that word of the atrocities only leaked out when terrified civilians fled to the relative safety of Bulawayo or Botswana.

On 4 April 1983 the curfew in Inyathi and Nkosikasi was lifted, and before the end of the month it was also ended in the rest of Matabeleland North, bringing some relief to residents, particularly as it was accompanied by a change in tactics on the part of 5 Brigade itself, probably at the instigation of the government.

The food supply situation eased and civilians could try to resume a semblance of normal life, although some schools remained closed.

Five Brigade remained a dominating and intimidatory force in the area. Adults and schoolchildren were forced to attend huge Zanu-PF (Zimbabwe African National Union – Patriotic Front) rallies, which frequently involved public beatings and lasted for entire weekends.

As a result, it became a matter of personal safety to own a

179

Zanu-PF card. Since most of the people in the region either carried Zapu cards or no political card at all, the purchase of Zanu-PF cards became a massive undertaking. Hundreds of people queued daily at Zanu-PF offices, where officials often made them wait overnight, forcing them to sing songs praising Zanu-PF and denouncing Zapu.

The fact that this new allegiance to Zanu-PF was a protective measure rather than a genuine political gesture on the part of locals was clearly indicated in the general election and the district council election of 1985, when Zapu was resoundingly returned in Matabeleland North.

From the end of March 1983, 5 Brigade became far more selective in terms of who it beat and killed. The phenomenon of mass beatings that had been so widespread was replaced by a policy of removing chosen villagers to central 5 Brigade camps where they were beaten, interrogated or killed.

Five Brigade was withdrawn from Matabeleland North for about a month in mid-1983, for a 'retraining exercise'. However, in July, before its departure, its members burnt 22 villagers to death, including women and children, in a hut in Solonkwe, a small village in western Tsholotsho.

On 29 August the brigade was redeployed in the area and resumed its activities for the remainder of 1983 and 1984. A doctor at St Luke's Hospital in Lupane noted that during the month of 5 Brigade's absence she admitted no patients with gunshot wounds, but once the brigade was redeployed, she started to see such cases again.

Throughout 1983, but particularly after March, there was an increase in 'disappearances': 5 Brigade and the Central Intelligence Organisation (CIO) removed men from buses, trains or from their homes, and they were never seen again. The victims were often selected because their names were on a list showing them to be either ex-Zipra (Zimbabwe People's Revolutionary Army), the armed wing of Zapu, or some kind of Zapu official, or because they had failed to produce their identity cards when pulled from a bus or train. Some who were killed or detained were merely young men considered to be of 'dissident age'.

The disappearances continued throughout the emergency period until unity in 1987, not only in Matabeleland North but also in Matabeleland South, where they were prevalent in 1984, and in the Midlands, where they coincided with the 1985 general elections. In February 1985 as many as 120 civilians in Tsholotsho are alleged to have been taken in night raids.

Five Brigade was finally withdrawn in 1985 and underwent conventional training in Nyanga under the guidance of a British military advisory team and instructors from the Zimbabwe national army.

One of the most tragic impacts of 5 Brigade on Matabeleland was the resulting perception among those civilians who suffered that they had become victims of an 'ethnic' and political war, with an attack on the Ndebele considered to be an attack on Zapu and an attack on Zapu seen as an attack on the Ndebele.

The incidence of rape under 5 Brigade also became loaded with political overtones for those in Matabeleland, with rapes committed by members of the brigade perceived as a means of creating a generation of Shona babies.

While peace returned to the rural areas of Matabeleland in the 1990s, many in the area feel alienated from the national body politic and believe that the area has been neglected in terms of development.

There is also a belief that a 5 Brigade-type onslaught could happen again at any time, particularly as the events of the 1980s have never been publicly acknowledged and no guarantees have been given that they will not be repeated.

Eyewitness reports

The following account of the Cewale River Massacre is by witness 2409 AG:

> On 5 March 1983 four people were taken from our home. The youngest was myself, then a girl of fifteen. The 5 Brigade took us – there were more than a hundred of them. We were

asleep when they came, but they woke us up, and accused the four of us – me and my three brothers – of being dissidents. They then marched us at gunpoint for about three hours until they reached a camp.

We were lined up and had to give our names before they took us to a building where there were finally 62 people. Then they took us out one by one and beat us. They beat me with a thick stick about 18 inches long all over the body. We were beaten until about 3 a.m.

Then the 5 Brigade marched us to the Cewale River, a few hundred meters away. All 62 of us were lined up and shot by the 5 Brigade. One of my brothers was killed instantly, from a bullet through his stomach. By some chance, seven of us survived with gunshot wounds. I was shot in the left thigh. The 5 Brigade finished off some of the others who survived, but my two brothers and I pretended to be dead.

After some time, we managed to get home. The 5 Brigade came looking for survivors of this incident at home – they found my brother R, who was badly injured, but they left him. My brother had a gunshot wound in the chest and arm, and later had to have his arm amputated first at the elbow, and then later at the shoulder. My brother had to have his foot amputated because of a bullet wound.

People found breaking the curfew regulations in any way

risked being shot, as the following testimony shows. The victim, a 39-year-old farmer (Case 762 X), was shot for riding a bicycle:

> At 6 a.m. on the morning of 13 February 1983, a Sunday, Mr N was cycling to St Luke's Hospital to visit his wife in the hospital. He met the 5 Brigade on the way. I, his brother, was informed on the afternoon of this day that a person who lived nearby had seen Mr N shot dead by 5 Brigade. The following morning I went with two friends to the spot where N lay dead near his bicycle. He had gunshots on the stomach. I wanted to bury N at my home, so we collected his body on the donkey cart. We were met by 5 Brigade on our way back and they saw N's body and the bicycle on the cart. They took the bicycle off the cart and broke it into pieces. They threatened me and my two friends with assault. We buried N at my home and I have had to raise and educate his three children who were all under ten when their father was killed.

At times, murders were not accompanied by mass beatings. Five Brigade would arrive at a village with a list of known members of the Zimbabwe National Army (ZNA), or demobbed ex-Zipras or deserters. If people on the list were found, they were shot. The following testimony, by the mother of victim 476 X, recounts such an instance:

184

At the end of January 1983, 15 members of 5 Brigade arrived in our line and came to our homestead. They split into two groups and searched our homestead and the homestead of another young ZNA member home on leave. They said they were looking for weapons which these two might have brought with them from the army when they came home.

They found nothing save personal clothing. They took my son out into the yard and told me, his mother, to go away. As I stood outside the yard, I heard a machine gun and they left. I got back to find my son riddled with bullets, with his chest shot wide open. We buried him.

They also shot our neighbour's son. He was made to sit near the house. He was shot in the chest and with two bullets in the head. We buried him. He was also home from the army on leave.

The following testimony, from witness 467 ASP, was made in western Tsholotsho, and is not untypical of 5 Brigade behaviour in this region. The alleged events occurred at the end of January 1983, within a day or two of 5 Brigade deployment:

The uniformed 5 Brigade soldiers arrived and ordered my husband to carry all the chairs, a table, bed, blankets, clothes and put them in one room. They also took all our cash – we had $1 500 saved, to buy a scotch cart. They then set fire to the hut and burnt all our property.

They accused my husband of having a gun, which he did not have. They shot at him. The first two times, they missed, but the third time they shot him in the stomach and killed him.

They then beat me very hard, even though I was pregnant. I told them I was pregnant, and they told me I should not have children for the whole of Zimbabwe. My mother-in-law tried to plead with them, but they shouted insults at her. They hit me on the stomach with the butt of the gun. The unborn child broke into pieces in my stomach. The baby boy died inside. It was God's desire that I did not die too. The child was born afterwards, piece by piece. A head alone, then a leg, an arm, the body – piece by piece.

A case of déjà vu: 'Operation makavhotera papi?'

On 29 March 2008 Zimbabwe held what were known as 'harmonised elections' – four elections in one day – local government, senatorial, parliamentary and presidential.[2] While the results of the parliamentary elections were announced over four days and reflected a resounding victory for the Movement for Democratic Change (MDC), the

186

presidential results were only released five weeks after election day and there was no clear winner – the MDC's Morgan Tsvangirai failed to receive the 50 per cent + one vote majority required for a clear win. As a result, a presidential run-off was scheduled for 27 June 2008.

The announcement on 2 May of the results of the presidential election unleashed an unprecedented wave of violence by Mugabe's supporters, including so-called war veterans, Zanu-PF youths, Zanu-PF councillors and traditional leaders, against supporters or suspected supporters of the MDC all over the country.

Cases of arson, murder and torture were reported in all provinces. In rural areas homes were torched and 'war veterans' allegedly killed cattle and other livestock belonging to opposition supporters. The violence resulted in the displacement of thousands of Zimbabweans, many of them women and children.

Senior Zanu-PF officials and some government officials were reported to have encouraged, funded and, in some cases, been directly involved in perpetrating the violence, even allegedly setting up bases designed to torture suspected opposition members in Mashonaland East and the Midlands.

Police turned a blind eye to many of these acts of political violence and, in some situations, actually arrested the victims. In their own operations police also raided the offices of several non-governmental organisations, including the Zimbabwe Election Support Network and the National Association of Non-Governmental Organisations, arresting senior officials.

The extent of the violence resulted in Morgan Tsvangirai withdrawing from the presidential run-off, unwilling to subject his supporters to further attacks. An account of how events unfolded thereafter is provided in Chapter 4.

NOTES

CHAPTER 1

This chapter is based on an expanded and revised version of
Moeletsi Mbeki. 2005. 'Perpetuating Poverty in Sub-Saharan Africa:
How African Political Elites Undermine Entrepreneurship and
Economic Development'. London: International Policy Press.
1 World Bank. 2000. *Can Africa Claim the 21st Century?*
Washington, DC: World Bank, p. 20.
2 Thandika Mkandawire. 2001. 'Thinking about Developmental
States in Africa'. *Cambridge Journal of Economics* 25, 3 (May):
289–313.
3 Lumumba's government was deposed in a coup after only ten
weeks in power. He was subsequently imprisoned and executed
in circumstances that remain murky.
4 Kwame Nkrumah was prime minister of the pre-independence
Gold Coast and post-independence Ghana from 1952–66
when his government was overthrown by a military coup,
which some claim was backed by the United States's Central
Intelligence Agency (CIA).

189

5 Odinga was placed under house arrest by President Daniel arap Moi in 1982 after a failed coup.

6 World Bank, *Can Africa Claim the 21st Century?*, p. 1.

7 Richard B. Freeman and David L. Lindauer. 1999. 'Why not Africa?' NBER (National Bureau of Economic Research) Working Paper 6942. Cambridge, MA.

8 Emily Wax. 2005. 'Driven Away by Upheaval, Drawn Back by Success'. *Washington Post*, 6 March.

9 Karl Marx. 1970. 'The Eighteenth Brumaire of Louis Bonaparte'. In Karl Marx and Friedrich Engels, *Selected Works in One Volume*. London: Lawrence and Wishart, pp. 170–71.

10 World Bank, *Can Africa Claim the 21st Century?*, Chapter 6. See also World Bank. 1981. *Accelerated Development in Sub-Saharan Africa*. Washington, DC: World Bank.

11 *The Economist*, 'People aren't Cattle', 17 July 2004. © The Economist Newspaper Limited, London, 17 July 2004.

12 Centre for the Study of African Economies. 2003 (unpublished). 'Sources of Growth in Nigeria: An Initial Analysis'. Oxford University.

13 Nancy Birdsall and Arvind Subramanian. 2004. 'Saving Iraq from its Oil'. *Foreign Affairs*, New York, July–August, pp. 77–89.

14 *The Economist*, 'Where are the Patients?', 21 August 2004.

15 *The Economist*, 'What Oil can do to Tiny States', 25 January 2003.

16 See www.redorbit.com/news/general/17545/uganda (accessed on 24 April 2009).

17 UN Office for the Coordination of Humanitarian Affairs. 2004. 'Equatorial Guinea: US Senate Probe Reveals Massive Theft of Oil Revenue', 16 July. And see, *Mail & Guardian*, 30 July 2004.

18 Eboe Hutchful. 2002. *Ghana's Adjustment Experience: The Paradox of Reform*. Oxford: United Nations Research Institute for Social Development, pp. 6, 81–82.

19 UNIDO (United Nations Industrial Development Organization). 2004. 'Industrialization, Environment and the Millennium Development Goals in Sub-Saharan Africa: The New Frontier

in the Fight against Poverty'. Vienna: Industrial Development Report, pp. 39–40.

20 Thandika Mkandawire and Charles Soludo. 2003. 'Our Continent, Our Future: African Perspectives on Structural Adjustment'. Discussion Paper no. 284. Ottawa: International Development Research Centre.

21 For Zimbabwe, see Figure 4.5 on page 123. With regard to South Africa's manufacturing sector, see André Roux. 2002. *Everyone's Guide to the South African Economy*. Cape Town: Zebra Press,
p. 56.

22 See kumekucha.blogspot.com/2006/07/exposed-murder-of-mboya-jm-and-ouko.html (accessed on 7 May 2009).

CHAPTER 2

Parts of this chapter draw on Moeletsi Mbeki. 2005. 'A Growing Gap between the Black Elite and the Black Masses?: Elites and Political and Economic Change in South Africa since the Anglo Boer War'. See vryeafrikaan.co.za/lees.php?%20id=267 (accessed on 7 May 2009).

1 Andrew Asheron. 1969. 'Race and Politics in South Africa'. *New Left Review* 53: 55–67.

2 'Order of the Baobab in Silver for a Pragmatic Pioneer', Business Day, 9 April 2009.

3 The amaMfengu are Xhosa-speaking people, called Fingo by the colonialists. The men of the amaMfengu were the first male Bantu speakers in southern Africa to become agriculturalists.

4 Ngqika became paramount chief of the Rharabe Xhosa when still a minor and his uncle, Ndlambe, ruled as regent. After Ngqika came of age Ndlambe led a group of dissidents in a revolt against him. In 1818 Ndlambe and his allies defeated Ngqika, who appealed for help from the British. The government sent an army to his assistance, defeated his enemies, and forced them to acknowledge Ngqika as

191

    paramount chief. In return, Ngqika ceded a large area of
    territory to the British.

5 The Glen Grey Act was introduced by Cecil Rhodes with the
    aim of stimulating the flow of labour to white farms. The story
    has been told most ably by others, among them: Colin Bundy.
    1979. *The Rise and Fall of the South African Peasantry*. London:
    Heinemann; Govan Mbeki. 1964. *South Africa: The Peasants
    Revolt*. London: Penguin African Library; Eddie Roux. 1964.
    Time Longer than Rope. Madison, WI: University of Wisconsin
    Press; and Tom Lodge. 1983. *Black Politics in South Africa since
    1945*. London: Longman.

6 See Revd James Dwane's evidence to the South African Native
    Affairs Commission 1903–05, Vol. 2, para 9695.

7 House of Commons. South African Native Affairs Commission
    1903–05, Vol. 3, para 25787.

8 Anthony Sampson. 1999. *Mandela: The Authorised Biography*.
    Johannesburg: Jonathan Ball Publishers, p. 95.

CHAPTER 3

Parts of this chapter originated as a public lecture, 'Concepts of
Transformation and the Social Structure of South Africa', presented
as one of the Wits Vice-Chancellor's Lecture Series, 26 April 2006.

1 Colin Bundy. 1979. *The Rise and Fall of the South African
    Peasantry*. London: Heinemann.

2 *Business Day*, 13 August 2004.

3 See www.transparency.org/policy_research/surveys_indices/cpi
    (accessed on 7 May 2009).

4 'The ruling ideas are nothing more than the ideal expression
    of the dominant material relationships, the dominant material
    relationships grasped as ideas; hence of the relationships which
    make the one class the ruling one, therefore, the ideas of their
    dominance.' From Karl Marx and Frederick Engels. 2001. *The
    German Ideology Part One, with Selections from Parts Two and
    Three, together with Marx's 'Introduction to a Critique of Political
    Economy'*. New York: International Publishers, p. 64.

5 Ben Fine and Zavareh Rustomjee. 1996. *The Political Economy of South Africa: From Minerals-Energy Complex to Industrialisation.* Johannesburg: Wits University Press.

6 Sampie Terreblanche. 2002. *A History of Inequality in South Africa, 1652–2002.* Pietermaritzburg: University of Natal Press.

7 Fine and Rustomjee, *The Political Economy of South Africa*, p. 8.

8 Francis Wilson. 1972. *Labour in the South African Gold Mines, 1911–1969.* Cambridge: Cambridge University Press.

9 Karl Marx. 1971 [1859]. Preface to *A Contribution to the Critique of Political Economy.* London: Lawrence and Wishart.

10 *Financial Times*, 7 October 2005.

11 In founding his institute Booker T. Washington had three central aims: to train teachers; to develop craft and occupational skills to equip students for jobs in the trades and agriculture; and to make Tuskegee what he called a 'civilizing agent'.

12 UNDP (United Nations Development Programme). 2003. *South Africa Human Development Report 2003.* Cape Town: Oxford University Press.

13 The emergence of the black elite has been extensively discussed by Terreblanche in *A History of Inequality in South Africa*, Chapter 2. See also Stephen Gelb. 2003. *Inequality in South Africa: Nature, Causes and Responses.* Johannesburg: The Edge Institute.

14 UNDP. 2005. *South Africa Human Development Report 2005.* Cape Town: Oxford University Press.

15 *Financial Mail*, 12 December 2005.

16 GEM (Global Entrepreneurship Monitor). 2003. *Global Report.* Cape Town: University of Cape Town Graduate School of Business, p. 9.

CHAPTER 4

1 Geoff Hill. 2003. *The Battle for Zimbabwe: The Final Countdown.* Cape Town: Zebra Press, p. 126.

2 Martin Meredith. 2002. *Robert Mugabe: Power, Plunder and Tyranny in Zimbabwe*. Johannesburg: Jonathan Ball, p. 148.
3 Hill, *The Battle for Zimbabwe*, p. 95.
4 For a useful exposition on Zimbabwe's land issues see Sam Moyo. 1995. *The Land Question in Zimbabwe*. Harare: SAPES Books.
5 Address by then Deputy President Thabo Mbeki to the Corporate Council on Africa's 'Attracting Capital to Africa' Summit. Chantilly, Virginia, 19–22 April 1997. See www.anc. org.za/ancdocs/history/mbeki/1997/sp970419.html (accessed on 28 April 2009).
6 Nandile Mgubentombi. 2004. 'South Africa's Foreign Policy towards Swaziland and Zimbabwe'. In SAIIA (South African Institute of International Affairs), *South African Yearbook of International Affairs 2003/04*. Johannesburg: SAIIA, pp. 145–57.
7 Physicians for Human Rights. January 2009. *Health in Ruins: PHR Reports on the Man-Made Health Crisis in Zimbabwe*. Cambridge, MA.
8 Physicians for Human Rights, *Health in Ruins*, p. 13.
9 Physicians for Human Rights, *Health in Ruins*, p. 13.
10 Hill, *The Battle for Zimbabwe*, p. 183. Also see the website of the Zimbabwe Election Support Network for reports on successive elections, www.zesn.org.zw (accessed on 7 May 2009).
11 Tom Burgis. 2009. 'Harare Power-Sharing Comes under Fire'. *Financial Times*, 8 March.

CHAPTER 5

1 UNHCR (United Nations High Commissioner for Refugees). *Statistical Yearbook* (various years). See www.unhcr.org/statistics (accessed on 8 May 2009).
2 See ghanaweb.com/GhanaHomePage/features/artikel. php?ID=100492 (accessed on 8 May 2009).
3 See www.afdb.org/fileadmin/uploads/afdb/Documents/Project-and-Operations/ADB-BD-WP-2004-110-EN-SOUTHERN-

AFRICA-REGIONAL-ASSISTANCE-STRATEGY-PAPER.PDF
(accessed on 8 May 2009).

4 Commission for Africa. 2005. *Our Common Interest: Report of the Commission for Africa*. London: Commission for Africa, p. 114.
5 See African Development Bank, OECD (Organisation for Economic Co-operation and Development) Development Centre and Economic Commission for Africa. 2007. *African Economic Outlook 2007*. Paris: OECD, pp. 574–75 (Table 1: Basic Indicators).
6 See Study South Africa, www.studysa.co.za/contentpage. aspx?pageid=4152 (accessed on 8 May 2009).

CHAPTER 6

1 Paul Collier. 2007. *The Bottom Billion: Why the Poorest Countries are Failing and What Can Be Done About It*. Oxford: Oxford University Press, pp. 4–5. (By permission of Oxford University Press, Inc.)
2 Susan E. Rice and Stewart Patrick. 2008. *Index of State Weakness in the Developing World*. Washington, DC: The Brookings Institution.
3 With its tiny population, a mere 82 247, Seychelles is not a significant player.
4 Karl Marx and Friedrich Engels. 1970. 'The Manifesto of the Communist Party'. In Karl Marx and Friedrich Engels. *Selected Works in One Volume*. London: Lawrence and Wishart, p. 37.
5 Marx and Engels, 'The Manifesto of the Communist Party', p. 37.
6 Michael Spicer. 2009. 'Nation at Crossroads as New Realities Cast Long Shadow'. *Business Day*, 27 January.
7 IISS (International Institute of Strategic Studies). 2007. *The Military Balance 2007*. London: IISS.
8 Chen Xiwen. 2000. 'Reform of Economic Structure in China's Rural Areas'. In Wang Mengkui, ed. *China's Economic Transformation over 20 Years*. Beijing: Foreign Languages Press, pp. 197–264.

9 Graph reproduced in Jeremy Seekings and Nicoli Nattrass. 2006 *Class, Race, and Inequality in South Africa*. Pietermaritzburg: University of KwaZulu-Natal Press, p. 383.
10 Luis Martinez (translated by Jonathan Derrick). 1998. *The Algerian Civil War 1990–1998*. London: Hurst and Company.
11 Michael B. Yahuda. 1978. *China's Role in World Affairs*. London: Taylor and Francis, p. 125.

APPENDIX

1 The information in this Appendix is drawn from a report prepared by the Catholic Commission for Justice and Peace in Zimbabwe. March 1997. 'Report on the 80s Atrocities in Matabeleland and the Midlands'. See www.newzimbabwe.com/pages/gukurahundi.html (accessed on 30 April 2009).
2 'Makavhotera papi?' translates as 'Where did you put your vote?' Information for this section of the Appendix is drawn from a report of the Zimbabwe Peace Project. May 2008. 'Post March 29th 2008 Elections Violence Report No. 1'. See www.humansecuritygateway.info/documents/ZPP_postelection.pdf (accessed on 30 April 2009).